Buchanan

CAUGHT IN THE CROSSFIRE

Buchanan

CAUGHT IN THE CROSSFIRE

GEORGE GRANT

THOMAS NELSON PUBLISHERS
Nashville • Atlanta • London • Vancouver

Published in Nashville, Tennessee, by Thomas Nelson, Inc., Publishers, and distributed in Canada by Word Communications, Ltd., Richmond, British Columbia, and in the United Kingdom by Word (UK), Ltd., Milton Keynes, England.

Unless otherwise noted, all Scripture quotations are from the NEW KING JAMES VERSION of the Bible, © 1979, 1980, 1982 by Thomas Nelson, Inc., Publishers.

Scripture quotations noted ASV are from The Holy Bible, AUTHORIZED STANDARD VERSION.

ISBN 0-7852-7255-0

Printed in the United States of America

1 2 3 4 5 6 7 — 00 99 98 97 96

To
Jim Smith
A Friend In Deed

and

To
Tom Clark
A Friend Indeed

Contents

Acknowledgments

No other success in life—not being President, or being wealthy, or going to college, or anything else—comes up to the success of the man and woman who can feel that they have done their duty and that their children and grandchildren rise up to call them blessed.

—*Theodore Roosevelt*[1]

Reflecting on the making of significant books, Francis Bacon once mused, "Histories make men wise; poets, witty; mathematics, subtle; natural philosophy, deep; morals, grave; logic and rhetoric, able to contend."[2] Notable for its absence from his list is political journalism. Perhaps that is because the Machiavellian arts can only make men even more Machiavellian. Despite that inherent danger, I have always found this particular genre both telling and compelling.

Thankfully, a number of kind friends and respected colleagues have encouraged me in that estimation. Especially in the context of this hurried project, they were immeasurably helpful. In particular, Howard Phillips, David Drye, Phil Hibbard, Tom Clark, David Shepherd, Ron Pitkin, and John Sanders urged me to write this

ACKNOWLEDGMENTS

book—and then prodded me onward in those moments when my efforts and enthusiasm began to flag.

Various members of the Buchanan campaign were kind enough to provide me with a steady supply of interviews, access to files, and late-breaking news. Larry Pratt, Rabbi Yehuda Levin, Steve Long, and Linda Muller were especially generous with their time and their expertise. In addition, the kind men and women of the Alan Keyes campaign were of inestimable help as well. Their faithfulness, courage, and selflessness are a model of Christian decorum.

Robert Wolgemuth, who first suggested this project, and Ken Stephens, who immediately recognized its value, were both incredibly supportive. They were there when I needed them—but they also gave me the time and space necessary to complete the job.

My co-laborers at the Franklin Classical School and my friends at the King's Meadow Study Center cheerfully tolerated my hurried inattention to details. Meanwhile, they took care to ensure that while I worried over such ephemera as looming deadlines, matters of much greater import were not altogether neglected. I am thus grateful for the faithfulness and diligence of all our board, staff, volunteers, and educators—Robert Fulcher, Gwen Smith, Ann Baumgartner, Marijean Green, Terry Cost, Tom Moucka, Terry Hendrixson, Karen Costello, Greg Wilbur, Judy Lowery, Sharon Taylor, Luann Redding, and Sylvia Singleton among many others.

The windface sound track for this project was provided by Steve Green, Craig Smith, Deanta, and Anuna while the fireface sound track was provided by James Horner, Patrick Doyle, and Michael Nyman. The moonlight musings were provided by John Buchan, Andrew Nelson Lytle, G. K. Chesterton, and Stephen Mansfield. Great thanks are due to them all.

As always, the completion of this work depended, in the end, upon the gracious ministrations of my beloved family. How they put up with me—and the crazy schedule projects like this impose upon our lives together—I'll never know. But I'm glad they do.

To all these I render heartfelt thanks and appreciation.

Though a book such as this may not make a man wise or witty—as Bacon might well argue—it is my prayer that it will at the very least offer readers a glimmer of insight into the tumultuous times in which we live. If it does that, then perhaps the investment of so many of these friends will not have been for naught.

King's Meadow Farm
First Day of Spring, 1996

Introduction

*It is not always easy to keep the just middle, especially
when it happens that on one side are corrupt and
unscrupulous demagogues, and on the other side corrupt
and unscrupulous reactionaries.*

—Theodore Roosevelt[1]

Writing for the *Atlantic Monthly*, Steven Stark made a telling assessment of Patrick Buchanan's quixotic campaign for president. "Of all the candidates running this time on either side," he said, "Buchanan has the most potential to change our politics."[2] How can that possibly be? Because, he asserted, "Presidential politics has always been about more than simply winning elections."[3] He explained:

> It is one of the ironies of American political history that the vanquished in presidential campaigns often end up altering our politics more than the victors. Barry Goldwater may have carried only six states in 1964, but by stamping his brand of Sunbelt conservatism on the Republican Party, he changed it and eventually the country, causing a regional realignment. George McGovern lost in a landslide in 1972, but some of his campaign aides—

including Gary Hart and Bill Clinton—ended up playing a strong role in Democratic politics for more than two decades afterward.[4]

The conventional wisdom is that Buchanan's continuing quest, against all odds, to bring his populist message of the "new conservatism of the heart" to the American people is as lost a cause as his bid to become the Republican Party's presidential nominee.[5] But more astute observers—like Stark—believe that Buchanan and his fledgling grass-roots movement are actually harbingers of a rather turbulent political sea change—that in fact, they represent the most significant development in American cultural relations in recent memory.

Newsweek magazine argued that the future of the Republican Party could be summarized as little more than "Pat versus Stop Pat,"[6] While the *New York Times* asserted that his influence is likely to "demonstrate a remarkable capacity" to "cross party lines and ideological distinctives."[7] According to *U.S. News and World Report* the impact of Buchanan's ideas "may well be felt for generations to come."[8] The *New Yorker* has admitted that he has "precipitated a fundamental realignment of the conservative movement."[9]

Thus, syndicated columnist Mary McGrory opined that Buchanan has accomplished something like a "reversal of the political order" by "stealing the working class" and "upsetting the apple cart" of the "traditional governing alignments."[10] James Perry has warned, "Win or lose, he will be heard," and the political estab-

lishment "will be forced to deal with him."[11] And Gary
Bauer concluded that his campaign has "permanently,
and profoundly, changed the course of American politics."[12]

Thus, according to Paul Likoudis:

> The electrifying campaign of presidential candidate Pat-
> rick J. Buchanan is not only sending panic through the
> ranks of Republican Party operatives and their hangers-
> on in the salons of neo-conservative policy wonks—it
> also has the potential of causing the most significant re-
> alignment of the national landscape in over 100 years.[13]

Despite the fact that he has been vociferously dismissed by the Republican Party establishment, denied
the presidential nomination by its monolithic political
machine, and derided as an extremist by its allies in the
mass media, Buchanan continues to define the terms of
the political debate—and the issues he has raised dominate the political landscape.[14]

Newspapers around the country headlined an Associated Press story following his surprise New Hampshire
primary victory asserting, "Let Republican history be
your guide: today's extremist often becomes tomorrow's
mainstream."[15] Indeed, as *Time* magazine quipped, "In
politics, a sure sign of a serious candidacy is when the
candidate finds himself at the bottom of a political pile-
on."[16]

This book is a brief examination of this phenomenon-
in-the-making. Its purpose is to identify just what it is

that Pat Buchanan is saying—and why it has struck such a nerve with friend and foe alike. It is thus more of a profile of Buchananism than it is of Buchanan—though admittedly, the man and the message are rather difficult to separate.

In the first two chapters, the background of the current maelstrom of ideas and personalities is surveyed—including an analysis of the dismal mood of American voters and a brief biographical sketch of the man who seems to epitomize that mood. The next three chapters deal with the issues Buchanan has raised throughout his career—allowing him to speak for himself as much as possible, but also giving ample room for his fiercest critics to sound off as well. The last chapter offers an estimation of the long-term effects of Buchanan and his ideas on American civilization.

Marred by name-calling, mudslinging, character assassination, and brazen innuendo, American political discourse has become a crass exercise in prejudice and intolerance. The more things change, the more they stay the same.

In 1838 James Fenimore Cooper introduced his prescient book of political analysis, *The American Democrat*, saying:

This little work has been written, in consequence of its author's having had many occasions to observe the manner in which principles that are of the last importance to the happiness of the community, are getting to be confounded in the popular mind. Notions that are impracticable, and which if persevered in, cannot fail to produce disorganization, if not revolution, are widely prevalent, and while many seem disposed to complain, few show a disposition to correct them. In those instances in which efforts are made to resist or to advance the innovation of the times, the actors take the extremes of the disputed points, the one side looking as far behind it, over ground that can never be retrod, as the other looks ahead, in the idle hope of substituting a fancied perfection for the ills of life.[17]

He went on to say: "It is the intention of this book to make a commencement towards a more just discrimination between truth and prejudice. With what success the task has been accomplished, the honest reader will judge for himself."[18]

Frankly, I could not hope for anything more for this little corban volume. Eliminating prejudice in our current harum-scarum environment would, of course, be no mean feat—but it is a feat we must all strive to accomplish.

PART I

Grand Old Populist

It is not the critic that counts; not the man who points out how the strong man stumbles, or where the doer of deeds could have done better. The credit belongs to the man who is actually in the arena, whose face is marred by dust and sweat and blood; who strives valiantly, who errs, and comes short again and again, because there is no effort without error and shortcoming; but who does actually strive to do the deeds.

—*Theodore Roosevelt*[1]

CHAPTER 1

Out of the Doldrums

I wish to preach not the doctrine of ignoble ease but the doctrine of the strenuous life; the life of toil and effort; of labor and strife; to preach that highest form of success which comes not to the man who desires mere easy peace but to the man who does not shrink from danger, hardship, or from the bitter toil, and who out of these wins the splendid ultimate triumph.

—*Theodore Roosevelt*[2]

To hear some political pundits talk these days, the three words they fear most are "Go, Pat, go." And Patrick Buchanan has apparently felt little inclination to allay their fears. Thus, he told an enthusiastic throng of supporters that: "They hear the shouts of the peasants from over the hill. You watch the establishment. All the knights and the barons will be riding into the castle, pulling up the drawbridge. They're coming. All the peasants are coming with their pitchforks."[3]

The problem is, knights and barons rarely cower inside their citadels of safety. They usually fight back. They overcome their initial fears. They muster their superior resources. And they almost always win. As Sidney Blumenthal has observed, "Peasant revolts tend to end in tragedy."[4]

Thus, just after Pat Buchanan's dramatic victory in New Hampshire's Republican primary, the *Boston Globe* predicted, "Buchanan is about to be repudiated by the barons of the party he's served for decades. It won't be pretty."[5] It has been, indeed, anything but pretty.

Buchanan tried to warn his supporters that things could get rather nasty. In his New Hampshire victory speech, he prophesied that the knights and barons—the establishment minions of politics-as-usual from both parties—were certain to rally and retaliate: "We no longer have the element of surprise. They're going to come after this campaign with everything they've got."[6]

According to syndicated columnist John McManus:

> Before the echo of Buchanan's words had faded, the political establishment, and its controlled media in the US and abroad, took up the chorus of defamation against Buchanan and his supporters. And prominent among the defamers were members of Buchanan's own Republican Party.[7]

So for instance, supply-side guru Jack Kemp dismissed Buchanan's victory, claiming that it "was based on fear."[8] Virtues czar William Bennett urged Republicans to fight "Buchananism" by throwing their support behind former Tennessee governor Lamar Alexander. Majority Whip Tom DeLay called Buchanan's economic policies "poison."[9]

Colin Powell accused him of "intolerance."[10] Rudolph Giuliani—the erstwhile Republican mayor of New York who threw his support to Mario Cuomo in the most recent gubernatorial race—condemned Buchanan for his supposed "racism and anti-Semitism."[11] And rival Steve Forbes argued that Buchanan had merely "tapped into a vein of fear and uncertainty." He then went on to compare him with Louis Farrakhan.[12]

And that was hardly the worst of it.

Columnist and television commentator George Will said of him: "The brawling barkeep from the Bowery of American politics, mixes a cocktail of resentments and ignorance unmatched since George Wallace went marauding."[13]

Bill Kristol, a former staffer for Dan Quayle and publisher of the *Weekly Standard*, went so far as to threaten to bolt the Republican Party altogether if Buchanan were actually to gain the nomination.[14] In addition, he said: "He is constitutionally opposed to the pieties that help make civil discourse civil. He has a natural, voracious, and often frightening appetite for the farthest edges of acceptable public debate."[15]

Lamar Alexander accused him of attempting to "hijack" the Republican Party.[16] And the reeling Republican front-runner, Robert Dole, declared that the campaign was now a battle of "mainstream versus extreme."[17]

Suddenly it seemed that all the knights and barons were rallying in an attempt to bury Buchanan beneath a blizzard of buzzwords: "anti-Semite, bigot, neo-fascist, extremist, nativist, isolationist, and racist."[18]

But despite his opponents' best efforts, Buchanan had struck a chord with ordinary Americans. Nearly 40 percent of rank and file Republicans think he has "the right answers to the country's problems."[19] With only a fraction of the money available to the other candidates and with the full party apparatus opposing him, he has still garnered strong grass-roots support that crosses all socio-economic boundaries.

Though the nomination has eluded him, he has undoubtedly captured the heart and soul of the party. According to *Time* magazine:

> Even more important than dollars or polls is the emerging sense that Buchanan is setting the pace in this race. He's the one with the resonant message; he's the one with the most passionate following. And most telling of all, he's the one the other candidates have started to copy. Pat Buchanan is fast becoming the Perot of 1996, the maverick with a message, who probably can't win but certainly won't go away. Listen to the other candidates, and it is easy to conclude that Buchanan has, in one sense, already won.[20]

When Bob Dole or Bill Clinton denounce "Hollywood sleaze-mongers," when they talk about "fair trade" as opposed to "free trade," and when they flirt with the notions of "welfare reform," the "flat tax," and a "review of congressional pension," they are merely lip-synching the Buchanan theme song.[21] They are responding to the very real and substantial appeal of his message.

According to political scientist Bernard Goldstein, this surprising populist appeal is due in part because "Most Americans are tired of politics as usual."[22] They are tired of the way the knights and barons have run the show for the past several years. And they are tired of living with the devastating results. "They see Pat Buchanan as a breath of fresh air" in the stuffy world of politics—a man who actually means what he says and says what he means.[23]

As *The Economist* succinctly put it: "Buchanan stands for something. He is the only one among the candidates now seriously in the chase who can plausibly lend his name to an 'ism.' "[24]

Clearly, the peasants like that.

Politics-as-Usual

The heroine of *My Fair Lady*, Eliza Doolittle, captured the sentiment of most American voters when she complained: "Words, words, words—I am so sick of words. I get words all day through, first from him, now from you. Is that all you blighters can do?"[25]

The empty rhetoric of politics-as-usual is simply no longer sufficient. Talk is cheap. Political promises are a dime a dozen. The electorate has just about had all of the spin-controlled sound bytes, indiscriminate mudslinging, and photo-op event-staging it can stand.

That is the message people have been sending the knights and barons again and again—at least since the mid-term elections of 1966. For the most part, it has been an unwaveringly negative message. Thus, they have voted, *inter alia, against* LBJ, *against* McGovern, *against* Nixon, *against* Carter, *against* Mondale, *against* Dukakis, *against* Bush, and most recently in the congressional elections, *against* Clinton.

Time after time they have voted *against* big government, *against* vested interests, *against* lumbering bureaucracies, *against* tenured elites, *against* ever-higher taxes, *against* meddlesome regulation, *against* promiscuous entitlements, and *against* amoral social engineering. They have sent a clear signal to the politics-as-usual establishment that they are *against* declining schools, decaying cities, and diminished expectations. They have asserted their wills *against* the assault on traditional values, families, churches, and small businesses.[26]

The chaplains of the knights and barons in the media have tried to write off the negative mood of the American people as a temporary phenomenon—a passing flirtation with a cranky anti-incumbency, a curmudgeonly populism, and a contrarian idealism fueled by fulsome talk radio and angry-white-male disillusionment. But such an analysis is woefully inadequate. Most folks are only too aware that our culture is in serious decline and something must be done—and done quickly. Their long-standing opposition to the machinations of politics-as-usual is actually rooted in a sober realization that we are in trouble. Real trouble.

By almost any standard, it appears that our culture is now coming apart at the seams. Despite all our prosperity, pomp, and power, the vaunted American experiment in liberty seems to be disintegrating before our very eyes.

According to historian Hilaire Belloc: "It is often so with institutions already undermined: they are at their most splendid external phase when they are ripe for downfall."[27]

How true. Even amidst all our comfort and affluence we have become a nation of mayhem and woe.[28] Crime is up. Educational standards are down. Families are crumbling. Basic virtues are disappearing. Government is less reliable. Scandal is more common. Our communities are sundered by antagonistic interests and competing factions. We are divided racially. We are divided economically. We are divided politically. We are divided culturally.[29]

And despite occasional flickers of hope here and there, things continue to worsen with every passing day.

According to the well-publicized and oft-quoted findings of *The Index of Leading Cultural Indicators*:

> The condition of our culture is not good. Over the last three decades we have experienced substantial social regression. Today the forces of social decomposition are challenging—and in some instances, overtaking—the forces of social composition. And when decomposition takes hold, it exacts an enormous human cost.[30]

And that exacting cost has all but devastated the American dream for ordinary working men and women —not just economically, but socially. They have for instance, watched in horror and disbelief as the number of illegitimate births has climbed 400 percent, as divorce rates have quadrupled, as the incidence of domestic violence has increased 320 percent, as the percentage of children either abandoned or left to their own resources has quintupled, and as teen suicides have skyrocketed 200 percent.[31] Meanwhile, those institutions that have traditionally provided stability, strength, and solace to ordinary families in times of crisis—our churches, private associations, and community organizations—have been systematically undermined. Their values have been attacked, their methods have been challenged, and their reputations have been distorted—more often than not at the hands of our own government and the social engineers under its aegis.

Amazingly, this assault was initiated under the pretense of *helping* us, not hurting us. Social spending by government has increased fivefold in the last thirty years.[32] Inflation-adjusted spending for the vast plethora of social service programs has increased 630 percent, while spending for its sundry educational programs has increased 225 percent.[33] But instead of helping matters, virtually every dollar poured into those programs has only made matters worse. The cure has turned out to be worse than the disease.

Thus, we are witnessing what Arthur Schlessinger calls the "disuniting of America."[34] Or worse, we are in the midst of what Daniel Patrick Moynihan pointedly calls "social and geo-political pandaemonium."[35]

Pundits and prognosticators, critics and commentators, gadflies and curmudgeons, prophets and seers alike agree. Aleksandr Solzhenitsyn says our "spiritual axis of life has grown dim."[36] Historian Simon Schama believes we are afflicted with "a deep and systemic sickness."[37] Speech-writing wiz Peggy Noonan thinks that "the vox has popped."[38] According to Henry Kissinger, we are in the midst of a "spiritual void."[39] Zbigniew Brzezinski says we are simply "out of control."[40] And Paul Johnson asserts we are ensnared by "a moral and ethical folly" that we appear to be "helpless to correct."[41]

As Chuck Colson has noted, "The times seem to smell of sunset."[42]

We are more divided today than at any time since the twin calamities of the War Between the States and Reconstruction. We are divided over what is right and what is wrong.[43] We are divided over what is good and what is bad.[44] We are divided over what we should do and what we should not do.[45] And as a result, "absolute confusion" is now our most apt epithet according to demographer George Barna.[46]

Os Guinness has sagely observed:

Under the conditions of late twentieth-century modernity, the cultural authority of American beliefs, ideals, and traditions is dissolving. Tradition is softening into a selective nostalgia for the past and transcendent faiths are melting into a suburbanesque sentiment that is vulnerable to the changing fashions of the therapeutic revolution. Thus with the *gravitas* of their cultural authority collapsing inward like the critical mass of an exploding star, parts of American society are beginning to flare out with the dazzling but empty brilliance of a great culture in a critical phase. The result is a grand loss of confidence and dynamism. As a result of much leveling, even more unraveling, and no little reveling in both, American beliefs, ideals, and traditions are fast becoming a lost continent to many Americans.[47]

Thus, Gertrude Himmelfarb argues that a prevailing demoralization has set in precisely because "We have succeeded in de-moralizing social policy—divorcing it from any moral criteria, requirements, or even expectations."[48]

James Michaels summarized all these provocative concerns for *Forbes* magazine:

It isn't the national debt or the unemployment rate or the current recession that bothers the nation's thinkers. It's not an economic mess that they see. It's a moral mess, a cultural mess. While the media natter about a need for economic change, these serious intellectuals worry about our psyches. Can the human race stand prosperity? Is the American experiment in freedom and equal opportunity morally bankrupt?[49]

Political scientist James Q. Wilson says: "What frustrates many Americans, I think, is that their hard-earned prosperity was supposed to produce widespread decency."[50]

It didn't. And as a result, they're mad.

They have resorted to negative politics out of self-defense. And while that is understandable, it is not necessarily commendable.

Patrick Henry once quipped:

It is far easier to agree on what we are against than it is to agree on what we are for. Opposition movements are a potent force for social change until it comes time to actually make the necessary changes. We all know what not to do. But knowing what we ought to do is another matter altogether. The negative is no replacement for the positive.[51]

A glib "just-say-no" or "throw-the-bums-out" attitude is not enough to effect genuine and lasting change. And yet, most Americans are somewhat at a loss to enunciate a thoroughly positive plan for the restoration of American society.

Pat Buchanan not only has been able to articulate the great concerns of average Americans, he has set forth that agenda for cultural renewal—an agenda that addresses the most fundamental issues facing them on a daily basis.

That he has, in turn, gotten them to actually engage in the political process, is no mean feat.

Anti-Politics

While E. J. Dionne may have exaggerated the case when he declared that "Americans hate politics," he was surely not too far astray.[52] For the most part, the electorate is rather unenthusiastic about the world of beltway policy wonks.

For most Americans, politics is important. But it is not all-important. That is not just a modern phenomenon. It has always been a fact of life.

Many who live and die by the electoral sword will certainly be shocked to discover that most of the grand-glorious headline-making events in the political realm today will go down in the annals of time as mere backdrops to the real drama of everyday banalities. But it is so.

As much emphasis as is placed on campaigns, primaries, caucuses, conventions, elections, statutes, administrations, surveys, polls, trends, and policies these days, most people know full well that the import of fellow workers, next-door neighbors, close friends, and family members is actually far greater. Despite all the hype, hoopla, and hysteria of sensational turns-of-events, the affairs of ordinary people who tend their gardens and raise their children and perfect their trades and mind their businesses are, in the end, more important. Just like they always have been. Just like they always will be.

That is the great lesson of American history. It is simply that ordinary people doing ordinary things are ultimately who and what determine the outcome of human events—not princes or populists issuing decrees. It is that laborers and workmen, cousins and acquaintances can upend the expectations of the brilliant and the glamorous, the expert and the meticulous. It is that simple folks doing mundane chores can literally change the course of history—because they are the stuff of which history is made. They are who and what make the world go round. As G. K. Chesterton has aptly observed, "The greatest political storm flutters only a fringe of humanity."[53]

Thus, what many presume to be electoral apathy is merely electoral ambivalence. It is not that the American people believe that politics is insignificant. It is just a recognition that in the end, there are any number of things in life that are *more* significant.

Most of us would have to agree with the astute political axiom of commentator George Will: "Almost nothing is as important as almost everything in Washington is made to appear. And the importance of a Washington event is apt to be inversely proportional to the attention it receives."[54]

Eugene McCarthy, once the darling of the New Left, also said it well: "Being in politics is like being a football coach; you have to be smart enough to understand the game, and dumb enough to think it's important."[55]

Intuitively, we know that is true. Thus, Alexis de Tocqueville for once was off the mark when he asserted that: "The very essence of democratic government consists in the absolute sovereignty of the majority: for there is nothing in democratic states which is capable of resisting it."[56]

Instead, we have to confess with the pundit, John Reston, that all politics is actually "based on the indifference of the majority."[57]

According to political analyst E. J. Dionne: "Americans view politics with boredom and detachment. For most of us, politics is increasingly abstract, a spectator sport barely worth watching."[58] He says that since the average voter "believes that politics will do little to improve his life or that of his community, he votes defensively," if at all.[59]

As odd as it may seem, that kind of robust detachment and nonchalant insouciance is actually close to what the Founding Fathers originally intended. They feared ongoing political passions and thus tried to construct a system that minimized the impact of factions, parties, and activists.[60] Citizens of the Republic were expected to turn out at the polls to vote for men of good character and broad vision—and then pretty much forget about politics until the next election.[61]

Gouverneur Morris—who actually wrote the first draft of the Constitution and was instrumental in its acceptance—said: "The Constitution is not an instrument for government to restrain the people, it is an instrument for the people to restrain the government—lest it come to dominate our lives and interests."[62]

Similarly, Patrick Henry stated:

Liberty necessitates the diminutization of political ambition and concern. Liberty necessitates concentration on other matters than mere civil governance. Rather, whatsoever things are true, whatsoever things are honest, whatsoever things are just, whatsoever things are pure, whatsoever things are lovely, whatsoever things are of good report; if there be any virtue, and if there be any praise, free men must think on these things.[63]

Suspicious of professional politicians and unfettered lobbyists as well as the inevitable corruptions of courtly patronage and special interests, the Founders established a system of severe checks and balances designed to depoliticize the arena of statecraft and its attendant statesmanship.[64]

Though there was disagreement between Federalists and Anti-Federalists about how much "energy," or "lack thereof," government ought to exercise, there was universal agreement about what John DeWitt called the "peripheral importance of institutional action to the actual liberties of daily life."[65]

Thus the Founders worked together to ensure that the republican confederation of states was free from ideological or partisan strife.[66]

Though they were not entirely successful, for much of our history American life has been marked by the distinct conviction that what goes on next door is of greater immediate concern than what goes on in Washington. Voter registration and turnout, for instance, have always been significantly lower here than in other free societies.

On average, only slightly more than half of the registered voters in the United States actually make it to the polls on election day.[67]

Belgium, Australia, Italy, Austria, Sweden, and Iceland all average over 90 percent participation, while Canada, Japan, Britain, Germany, France, Israel, Greece, New Zealand, Luxembourg, Portugal, Spain, Denmark, the Netherlands, and Norway each see over 70 percent.[68]

Although there was a brief and dramatic decline in what political scientists call the "metapolitics of participation" following the presidential election of 1896,[69] voter turnout percentages have otherwise remained remarkably constant throughout our history.[70]

Americans have rarely roused themselves sufficiently to get too terribly excited about their electoral choices. They generally have found something better to do than vote.

The most recent elections have proven to be no exception. Though the media mandarins have hailed "record turnouts"[71] and the "massive numbers,"[72] the actual percentage of eligible voters who cast their ballots has remained virtually unchanged from years past—a variation of plus or minus three points does not constitute a "surging trend" or a "clarion cry" from the electorate.[73]

If anything, it indicates their profound boredom with the whole affair. Thus, syndicated columnist Jane Lawrence was hardly exaggerating when she wrote:

Most Americans yawned their way through what turned out to be an unpleasant exercise in political obfuscation. Perhaps the reason they care more about PTA meetings, zoning hearings, and Rotary luncheons is that in the end, those things actually matter more. It is hard, after all to get enthusiastic about a choice between Tweedledee and Tweedledum—or to discern what difference such a choice might make.[74]

Not that any of this entirely justifies our tenured ambivalence. The fact is, at a time when government debt, spending, and activist intrusions into our families and communities have grown to almost incomprehensible Babylonian proportions, our *que sera sera* citizenship has offered the politics-as-usual bureaucrats and politicians in Washington tacit approval to lead us ever farther down the road to ruin. And so, with Pied Piper efficiency and aplomb, they have.

During similar times of distress in our nation's history—following the Jeffersonian and Jacksonian eras, immediately after Reconstruction and the Great War, and most recently on the heels of the New Deal and Great Society episodes—Americans have stirred themselves momentarily from their *laissez faire* political lethargy to rekindle the fires of freedom. In the face of impending disaster, the collapse of moral resolve, the encroachment of abusive power, and the abnegation of liberty, they committed their lives and their fortunes to the process of political restoration. They proved that one of the great ironies of the American system is that there are times when politics must be treated as a matter of some consequence so that it ceases to be treated as a matter of total consequence.

A New Populism

Despite the persistent evidence that we are now living in just such a time of clear and present danger, American disinterest in politics has only ossified and hardened with the passing of time. We have yet to rally. In fact, our belligerent ambivalence over the destructive antics of politics-as-usual may very well be the defining feature of our day.

But the campaign of Pat Buchanan has threatened to change that—thus, the ominous teeth-gnashing and the saber rattling of the knights and barons.

According to columnist John McManus:

As 1996 began, so did Buchanan's march to heightened respectability with voters and to renewed defamation by the "experts." He won in Alaska, delivered a knockout blow to Phil Gramm in Louisiana, rose to top-tier status with a strong finish in Iowa, and overcame an early 50 percentage-point deficit to defeat Bob Dole in New Hampshire. But even before his February 20th triumph in New Hampshire, the leading lights of the establishment media cranked up their invective machines and exceeded anything they had issued before.[75]

Nevertheless, his message is still hitting home. While other politicians find that their campaigns must struggle with apathy, half-filled halls, and lackadaisical support, Buchanan's grass-roots campaign still has a full head of steam.

According to columnist Paul Likoudis:

The crowds Buchanan draws and the enthusiasm he generates frighten the cerebrally challenged liberal pundits, who don't understand the deep chord Buchanan is striking in the hearts of America's middle class. In American politics, such passion has not been seen in 100 years, since the 1896 presidential race of populist William Jennings Bryan, a candidate who, like Buchanan, championed the cause of the "common man" against the robber barons and the imperialists. The populist candidate, then and now, is one who championed Main Street over Wall Street, who stood on the side of real people against the cruel theories that robbed them of their livelihood, their hope, and their faith. It is a voice that warns the republic of the danger of imperialism abroad and the financial chicanery at home, which upholds the Jeffersonian ideal of free and independent yeoman against the view of the effete elites who see the citizen as a customer to drive the market. Against all the considerable power of the powers-that-be, Buchanan is energizing voters from Boston to San Diego, and his message is "spreading like wildfire."[76]

This dramatic revival of this kind of American populism has been dubbed by Buchanan as the "new conservatism of the heart." It is in fact a revival of the "Old Right" values—of tight-knit communities, family-centered values, faith-derived virtues, work-ethic scruples, and international noninterventionism—that were sublimated by the New Deal, World War II, and the Cold War. Buchanan offers hope that such a traditional conservatism could very well become a major political force in the United States—because it combines two things: intellectual sophistication and mass appeal.

This sort of populism—which takes much of its indigenous inspiration from Thomas Jefferson, Andrew Jackson, John Calhoun, William Jennings Bryan, and Theodore Roosevelt—resonates with ordinary working men and women as well as with authentic intellectual conservatives who still believe that the principles of the Founding Fathers are relevant to American politics.

In the end, such a movement can only be perceived by the politics-as-usual establishment as a threat. As syndicated columnist Joe Sobran has written:

> Courage inspires some people and terrifies others. This explains the wild emotions Buchanan provokes on all sides; it even explains why he has so many conservative enemies. He has shown under great pressure that he simply doesn't back down. When he refused to dump an embattled aide recently, he showed loyalty and guts to a degree almost unknown in Washington. He not only frustrated his enemies; he shamed them. The vindictive nit-picking we are seeing in the press is the revenge of the nerds.[77]

He went on to assert that if any of the other candidates were to suddenly fold, no one would likely sing "His

truth is marching on." Their defeat would be final, "because they don't actually stand for anything beyond personal ambition." None of them can be described as "a
warrior in a larger cause, or as the embodiment of a
principle." None of them "inspires or scares anyone."
And none of them "would make any great difference
even by winning the presidency." But, he concluded:

> Buchanan has already won something lasting, even if he
> never wins the presidency. He has changed what we
> think of as politically possible, and even the way we will
> talk about politics hereafter. Whoever wins this year's
> race will be talking about the issues Buchanan has raised.
> His enemies are trying to turn his name into an epithet:
> "Buchananism" (as in "McCarthyism"). But this is plau-
> sible only because he represents something, whether you
> like it or not.[78]

Indeed, he argued, it would be absurd to speak of
"Dolism" or even of "Clintonism." "Buchananism,"
on the other hand, is a real and viable label because
Buchanan has real and viable ideas—ideas that have
shape and substance, "the din of negative farrago" not-
withstanding.[79]

Thus, according to Family Research Council president
and former Reagan staffer Gary Bauer, the Buchanan
populist surge affords us with six crucial lessons on the
future of American political life. First, he argues:

> From here on, the social and economic conservatives are
> on an equal footing. No more back-of-the-bus treatment

for the rank and file family folks. There has to be a single standard of action, not talk. For 15 years, social conservatives have been given rhetoric about their issues, while economic conservatives have gotten policy. Look at what the Senate GOP leadership is pushing right now: a regulatory moratorium, product liability reform, line item veto. All good things, but where's the social component? In canned speeches, that's where—until now.[80]

The popular surge of the Buchanan message, he says, now compels the Republican establishment to "deal with the moral decay that is the primary cause of everything from educational collapse to urban violence, from the drug plague to child abuse."[81]
Second, he says:

Weakness or unwillingness to take on the great moral issues of our day is a character issue for those who care deeply about the decay of our nation. Those who care about the breakdown of the family, our virtue deficit, and who mourn the cultural tragedies of out-of-wedlock births, educational failures, crime and the fate of the weakest members of society will reject those candidates who don't convey a willingness to act on these issues. Lip service will not cut it any longer. The great moral debates of our day must be met with a commitment to act, not just talk. Voters want a president who will lead, not just split the difference. For those motivated by matters of the heart, candidates whose moral convictions wobble on poll data are inherently untrustworthy. If streets are paved with gold but children are killing one another, we are not a wealthy country.[82]

According to Bauer the third crucial lesson Buchanan's "new conservatism of the heart" teaches us is that the "Big Tent" has fallen on hard times in the Republican Party:

It came crashing down when Republican leaders—including, incomprehensibly, the presidents of several DC-based think tanks—read Buchanan out of conservative ranks on the trade issue. After years of denouncing a hypothetical pro-life litmus test, many powerful Republicans now reveal one of their own: free trade. Sorry, guys. If we can't have one, neither can you. Or else, if you have yours, we get ours. Which will it be?[83]

The fourth lesson is that the sanctity of life is now a core political issue:

Try some simple math: Add Buchanan's 23 percent in Iowa with Alan Keyes' 7 percent. If the latter had not been in the race, with what is virtually a single-issue campaign, the pro-life issue would have handed Pat that state—and perhaps ended the race there and then. Sure, this profoundly ethical issue discomfits some of the GOP's most influential and well-heeled backers. But from here on out, the Party's soul cannot be for sale.[84]

Fifth, according to Bauer, the governing coalition must be the party of both Wall Street and Main Street:

We can't win without the support of millions of middle class Americans. Let's be blunt: Most social conservatives are strong economic conservatives as well. They want low taxes, deregulation and smaller government. But they're realistic about the shortcomings of Big Business. For example, they know how much of Planned Parenthood's cash comes from major corporations. They see the corporate giants play all sides of the political fence to ruthlessly advance their financial interests, pouring money into anti-family campaigns to buy access. Where was Wall Street on the $500 per child tax credit? Unless Big Business thinks it can cohabit in the Democratic house that Bill built, it had better clean up its act and come home to the majority coalition of which social conservatives are now the largest single element.[85]

Finally, he argues:

Social conservatives aren't owned by the GOP. Indeed, they're not even owned by social conservative leaders. No national organization—including our own—has been controlling the GOP race so far. On the contrary, pro-family activists have enlisted behind most of the GOP presidential contenders, seeing merits across the board. Now there's been a winnowing out, and millions of individual social conservatives are making their own prayerful decisions about the remaining candidates. Sounds like good citizenship to me.[86]

It may sound like good citizenship to him, but apparently, to the knights and barons of the politics-as-usual establishment, it sounds a bit more like "shouts from over the hill." It sounds like "all the peasants are coming with their pitchforks."[87]

CHAPTER 2

An American Life

Far better it is to dare mighty things, to win glorious triumphs, even though checkered by failure, than to take rank with those poor spirits who neither enjoy much nor suffer much because they live in the gray twilight that knows neither victory nor defeat.

—*Theodore Roosevelt*[1]

Patrick Buchanan comes by his family values honestly—he got them from his family. There is probably no more important fact to know about him than that. Almost everything that he is, everything that he does, and everything that he aspires to be is defined by the fundamental relationships cemented by the family bonds of blood and covenant.

Journalist Steven Stark has correctly stated:

Virtually everyone who writes about Buchanan, including himself, talks about his strong roots in the deeply religious and traditional Catholic enclaves of mid-century Washington: he comes from a family of eleven, was raised in Blessed Sacrament parish, attended Gonzaga High School, run by Jesuits, and Georgetown University as a day student. It was in this close-knit community that Buchanan was born and bred a brawler.[2]

His 1988 autobiography, *Right from the Beginning,* is notable for its emphasis on family, community, and faith.[3] There is no scrimping on the little details in order to hurry on to matters of some political import. In fact, reading it you get the distinct impression that it is actually the details that matter more than things of political import. Buchanan revels in the minutiae of life—for it is there that real life is lived.

Thus, Stark properly observes: "Although most books about politicians make short work of childhood to get to the politics, Buchanan's book has a terrible time leaving home."[4]

That is because Buchanan himself has a terrible time leaving home—it intrudes on every conversation, every issue, every project, and every campaign. And far from being a weakness, this is, in fact, his greatest strength. He is secure in who he is, what he is called to do, and what he must do to attain it, because he has the surest and securest foundation anyone could ever ask for: a happy upbringing.

Father

The third son of William and Catherine Buchanan, Patrick Joseph Buchanan was born on All Soul's Day, November 2, 1938. His mother was a nurse who continued to practice until her third child came along—taking midnight calls to go back into the inner city to minister to the sick, both black and white. His father was an up-and-coming accountant, who eventually established a flourishing private practice in Georgetown.

The family lived in a sleepy ethnic neighborhood—a quiet, pleasant place that has since disappeared. It was a wonderful time and place to grow up. The boys, all just a year apart, were inseparable. They were a happy, rowdy bunch that inevitably dominated the playgrounds and sidewalks around their block with exuberant play and clannish loyalty.

The precocious young "Paddy Joe" could talk before he could walk. And early on he showed great intellectual promise. When his brothers—still toddlers themselves—struggled over the words to their prayers, he impatiently finished their sentences for them from his perch in the playpen across the room.

For all the fun they had together and for all the adventures they shared in their neighborhood, the great dominating influence in the boys' life was their father. Abandoned as a child by his own father, William Buchanan determined to be an ideal husband and father. And he very nearly was.

He apparently had a voracious appetite for truth and was unapologetically opinionated. Politics was a particularly favored topic of discussion—at the dinner table, driving about town in his big red Dodge, reading through favorite newspaper columns, or just walking along the sidewalk in the neighborhood. He thus introduced his children to the world of ideas and their practical consequences.

Because he was a traditional Catholic, William had a particular fondness for those politicians who most stridently stood for the eternal values of justice, mercy, and piety. He didn't have much use for the flashy innovator or the messianic demagogue. He was an Al Smith Democrat who came to deeply distrust Franklin Roosevelt and his bureaucratic minions of the New Deal.

He apparently loved all the accoutrements of a large family—and he gathered his brood around him closely and affectionately. Reading stories at bedtime, gathering around the family radio, or participating in sports or family outings, he made sure that he was an integral part of their lives.

But he was also a stern disciplinarian who had little tolerance for bad manners, irresponsibility, or insubordination. Clearly, with his growing brood, he had his hands full.

Pat distinguished himself as more than a little belligerent. He loved to argue. According to his siblings, he was always stirring trouble—both at home and out in the neighborhood. The catalog of his fights, scraps, and tussles make up a substantial portion of his autobiography.

His father actually encouraged the boys to be tough, to be able to defend themselves and one another. He even cast a glance of knowing tolerance upon their often fierce sibling rivalry. Pat would later see this as an essential aspect of his childhood character-building.

Perhaps the greatest gift his father gave to him—and his brothers and sisters—was the gift of faith. William Buchanan naturally lived out the implications of his faith in virtually every area of his life. His was a fully integrated faith—able to withstand both trouble and blessing with the even-keel Christian virtue. In both tragedy and joy, he was a model to them all.

Brothers

Of his eight siblings, six were brothers. All followed an identical path from elementary school at the Blessed Sacrament parish school and then on to Gonzaga High School. Run by no-nonsense Jesuits, the high school was a training ground for both temporal character and eternal virtue. The priests were true educators—of the sort now nearly extinct.

The renowned Catholic educator of the previous generation, Leo Brennan, once asserted, "Though we don't have much to show for it, we Americans are enthusiasts for education."[5] What was true in his day was perhaps even more true when the Buchanan boys began attending Gonzaga. While there was an underlying "anti-intellectualism" in a few isolated circles, by and large Americans—and particularly American Christians—placed a heavy emphasis on the education of their children. They demanded good teachers. They demanded good textbooks. They demanded good facilities. They demanded good supplemental resources. They demanded the best and the latest and the snazziest of everything academia had to offer. Which made their profound lack of it all the more ironic.

The problem, argued Brennan, was that "we engage in the eminently dubious process of what is barbarously known as standardization." As a result, "we lower our ideals and we smear our philosophy" by playing "the sedulous ape" to popular "uniformitarian educational fads and fashions."[6]

The only solution, he said, was to "restore the basic educational ideals and principles" that provoked Christendom's great flowering of culture in the first place: a strident emphasis on serious and diverse reading, the use of classical methodologies, and all this integrated into the gracious environs of Christian family life.[7]

That was precisely what the Jesuits at Gonzaga had attempted to do—provide a solid classical education for the boys who attended their school.

So while the clannish Buchanan boys brawled and bruised their way through all the typical activities and distractions of teenage boys—from organized sports to disorganized carousing—they were simultaneously getting a rare opportunity to train their minds.

They were educated in a way that we can only dream of today despite all our nifty gadgets, gimmicks, and bright ideas. They were steeped in Augustine, Dante, Plutarch, and Vasari. They were conversant in the ideas of Seneca, Ptolemy, Virgil, and Aristophanes. The notions of Athanasius, Chrysostom, Anselm, Bonaventure, Aquinas, Machiavelli, Abelard, and Wycliffe informed their thinking and shaped their worldview.

The now carelessly discarded traditional medieval Trivium—emphasizing the basic classical scholastic categories of grammar, logic, and rhetoric—equipped them with the tools for a lifetime of learning: a working knowledge of the timetables of history, a background understanding of the great literary classics, a structural competency in Greek- and Latin-based grammars, a familiarity with the sweep of art, music, and ideas, a grasp of research and writing skills, a worldview comprehension for math and science basics, a principle approach to current events, and an emphasis on a Christian life paradigm.

The methodologies of this kind of classical learning adhered to the time-honored principles of creative visual, auditory, and tactile learning: an emphasis on structural memorization, an exposure to the best of Christendom's cultural ethos, a wide array of focused reading, an opportunity for disciplined presentations, an experience with basic academic skills, and a catechizing for orthopraxy as well as orthodoxy.

It was the modern abandonment of these classical standards that provoked G. K. Chesterton to remark:

The great intellectual tradition that comes down to us from the past was never interrupted or lost through such trifles as the sack of Rome, the triumph of Attila, or all the barbarian invasions of the Dark Ages. It was lost after the introduction of printing, the discovery of America, the coming of the marvels of technology, the establishment of universal education, and all the enlightenment of

Mentor #1: Goldwater

After the defeat of Richard Nixon in 1960, the conservative movement was in utter disarray. Its principles and primary heroes had been repudiated in every election since 1932. Even in the Republican Party, the last bastion of old-school values—faith, family, work, accountability, and decentralization—conservatives were a scorned minority voice. Joe McCarthy was gone—and now, even his memory was disgraced. And even the long-suffering Robert Taft was gone—and with him died the last conservative leader of national stature.

And then came Barry Goldwater.

In 1960, the little-known senator from the state of Arizona penned a slim volume entitled *The Conscience of a Conservative*. Almost immediately the small cadre of conservatives that remained were electrified. Like the man himself, the book was plain-spoken and unadorned. But in its simplicity was a profound awareness of what the Founding Fathers intended when they crafted this great experiment in liberty. It quickly became the college-student underground book of the times. Eventually more than four million hardback copies of the book were sold.

Pat Buchanan enlisted immediately in Goldwater's crusade to restore the Republic after three decades of New Deal liberalism and to recapture the Republican Party after three decades of Wall Street accommodationism. A twenty-three-year-old graduate student at Co-the modern world. It was there, if anywhere, that there was lost or impatiently snapped the long thin delicate thread that had descended from distant antiquity; the thread of that unusual human hobby: the habit of thinking.[8]

The Buchanan boys were among the last generation to receive that kind of comprehensive intellectual and spiritual training.

By the time he had reached college—he decided to stay at home and attend Georgetown University—Pat Buchanan was a confirmed classicist. He read widely and voraciously. Throughout all four years of high school and college, he never took a single course in political science. He gleaned his practical knowledge of civics from the literary works of Thucydides, Caesar, Machiavelli, Burke, and Hume.

While all this academic effort was taming and training his mind, he remained more than a little rambunctious in his behavior—always a fighter, he was involved in an altercation with police one night that resulted in his temporary expulsion from Georgetown. But through thick and thin, the most outstanding feature of his years in school was his relationship with his brothers. The bond that their father had sought to forge between them was ironclad.

It was a trait that each of the Buchanan boys would carry with them into all their future endeavors—and one that would particularly define the character and demeanor of Pat Buchanan.

lumbia University in New York, he was a right-wing oddity: a Goldwater zealot.

Ever since he was a little tyke at his father's knee, Buchanan was nurtured with a fascination with politics. His literary predilections—now fully blossoming in journalism school—seemed only to intensify his interests in campaigns and governance.

But it was with the Goldwater campaign that Buchanan began his practical political pilgrimage. With all the other idealistic volunteers from Young Americans for Freedom, he cut his teeth on the same campaign that ultimately launched Ronald Reagan into the national spotlight.

When John Kennedy was assassinated in 1963, Buchanan knew that all they had been working toward was now doomed. The mood of the country suddenly swung away from the principles of conservatism in a reaction of grief, anger, and dismay.

The bitter and crushing defeat of Goldwater in the 1964 presidential race sent most conservatives back to the caves. But it only stirred Buchanan's passions all the more. He was soon plotting his next move in support of the cause.

Through the entire ordeal, he learned a great deal— and was given the opportunity to get involved in the fledgling conservative movement from its genesis. It also meant that he would have lifelong associations that would serve him well as his career advanced in future years.

He would later write:

Like a first love, the Goldwater campaign was, for thousands of men and women now well into middle age, an experience that will never recede from memory, one on which we look back with pride and fond remembrance. We were there on St. Crispin's Day. I have never met an old Goldwaterite who thought that perhaps we should have gone with Rockefeller, Scranton, or Lodge. Because the cause seemed hopeless, because the crew-cut militants of the Goldwater movement were relentlessly demonized as racist and reactionary, there were few trimmers and time-servers in the all-volunteer Goldwater army. In those days, at least, the phrase "conservative opportunist" was a contradiction in terms.[9]

To this day, Buchanan seems to have yet to discover a way to resolve that contradiction—he remains anything but an opportunist.

Mentor #2: Nixon

Following the election debacle, there were only two visible national leaders left in the Republican Party. The first was George Romney, who had carefully distanced himself from Goldwater during the campaign. The other was Richard Nixon, who had campaigned for Goldwater as tirelessly as the candidate himself.

Buchanan decided that Nixon was the man to carry the torch of the old school. By this time, he had gotten his first job writing for the conservative *St. Louis Globe Democrat*. His talent was evident and he rose quickly through the ranks of that venerable paper. It was there that he honed his considerable prowess as a wordsmith.

In December 1965, Buchanan had an opportunity to meet Nixon—and in a hastily arranged midnight meeting in Illinois, he proposed to the former vice president that he "get on board early." The next year he did just that—and he remained a faithful staffer until Nixon left office in disgrace following Watergate.

Almost immediately Buchanan proved to be a valuable asset to the old political warrior. He seemed to have a combination of killer instinct and clear-eyed empathy for the common working man or woman. With another brilliant young strategist, Kevin Phillips, he devised the brilliant "southern strategy" for the campaign as well as its "silent majority" emphasis.

Through thick and thin, Buchanan remained loyal to Nixon. Though he avoided many of the Machiavellian machinations that ultimately undermined the administration, he remained a consummate insider to the end. In 1971, several senior White House staffers came to him with a great opportunity: They wanted him to head up an opposition research group—the Watergate plumbers. Buchanan turned them down cold. He told Charles Colson, H. R. Haldeman, and John Ehrlichman that he thought the idea was "stupid." In a bold memo to the men he wrote: "I have yet to be shown what benefits this would do for the president, or for the rest of us, other than a psychological salve. Right out in the open, that's our forte."[10]

Never much of one for subtlety, Buchanan believed in the truth—and that eventually the truth would prevail. Unfortunately, as he would later discover, that was a minority view in the Nixon White House.

Nixon was like a second father to him. So, when he discovered the full significance, the duplicity, and the corruption of the Watergate cover-up, he was not only angry, he felt utterly betrayed. He was instrumental in convincing the president to resign.

Though he stayed in the White House briefly to help with the transition for Gerald Ford, he began to look for career options outside the hurly-burly world of politics.

He secured a deal to write a syndicated column—and so began what turned out to be a very profitable career as a pundit. By 1978, he was appearing on a variety of television panel shows and was traveling the country as a speaker.

Mentor #3: Reagan

He returned to the White House to serve as Ronald Reagan's communications director from 1985 to 1987. By that time he had gained an independent reputation as a defender of the old conservative ideals—and as a no-holds-barred, take-no-prisoners orator.

He had long been a supporter and admirer of Ronald Reagan. In fact, shortly after leaving the Ford White House, he determined that Reagan was the future of the Republican Party. Early on, he threw his considerable weight behind Reagan's 1976 bid for the presidential nomination.

Many in the establishment wing of the party believed that Reagan would be another disaster for the GOP. He was accused—like Goldwater—of being an extremist. He was slandered and vilified.

The party—still reeling from Watergate—was simply not ready for a genuine conservative voice. But four long years of Jimmy Carter made it ready. And how.

During those years of exile, Buchanan honed his razor wit and lightning reflexes.

When Reagan finally won the nomination—and then went on to win the election handily—Buchanan was there, every step of the way. Twenty years after the publication of *The Conscience of a Conservative,* a Goldwater conservative was sworn in to the highest office in the land.

Initially, Buchanan was snubbed by the team Reagan surrounded himself with. Eventually, though, the administration ran afoul of the true conservatives, and Don Regan began casting about for a way to appease them. He decided to try to bring in Buchanan to supervise the president's speech-writing team. So began his stormy tenure as communications director in the White House.

Once again, Buchanan was fiercely loyal. But once again, his trust was betrayed. The Iran-Contra scandal broke shortly after he arrived on the job. And although he did his utmost to shore up support for Oliver North and other involved administration personnel, he began to get the sensation of *déjà vu.* After two frustrating years, Buchanan left the White House and returned to his journalistic enterprises.

His TV work now included two stints as co-host of CNN's *Crossfire* and as a regular panelist on *The Mc-Laughlin Group*. He quickly became the most outspoken advocate of constitutionalism and public integrity—so a number of his colleagues began to urge him to consider a run for the presidential nomination. Old friends from the Goldwater and Nixon years, such as Howard Phillips, began floating his name as a possible successor to Reagan.

Eventually, he decided to stick with his journalistic efforts—until 1992, when he simply could not restrain himself from getting into the fray any longer. *Crossfire* pitted opposing partisans of virtually every political and cultural issue against one another—with Buchanan prodding from the right and cohost Michael Kinsley on the left. The discussions were often quite lively—sometimes degenerating to little more than shouting matches. But according to James Brewster, a Republican political consultant, it uniquely prepared Buchanan for national public service:

> Buchanan became a kind of national spokesman for serious political issues. While Rush Limbaugh admittedly garnered a wider following, he was more often than not considered an entertainer. Buchanan on the other hand was a serious public policy analyst who actually had the courage to say what he meant. *Crossfire* made him a real player.[11]

Indeed it did. He met virtually every one, from every side, of every political social issue. As Brewster asserts, "There is probably no one in politics today who knows more of the movers and shakers across the whole spectrum of serious debate, than Buchanan."[12] Add that experience with his Nixon and Reagan White House stints, where he met and interacted with nearly every major world leader, and you have the makings for an extraordinary breadth and depth of understanding of the issues. And as Brewster points out: "Buchanan was always very conscientious in his preparation for meetings and interviews. He read every book, he did an enormous amount of research, and he made certain that he was well-informed by talking through every aspect of the issue at hand."[13]

Contrary to popular opinion, Buchanan was not an off-the-cuff pundit, but a carefully studied student of the issues of the day. When he gave up his column and his *Crossfire* slot to run for president in 1992, journalist Robert Scheer reported Buchanan was walking away from an annual income of $800,000. That is not an easy thing to do. But there were two things that made the decision much easier: his sister and his wife.

Women

Newsweek magazine asserted: "With his bullying persona and his total opposition to abortion, Pat Buchanan may well be public enemy No. 1 to many women political activists around the nation."[14]

Ironically, his actions belie his reputation. The fact is the two people who have the most influence over the candidate and his populist campaign are both women— his younger sister Bay and his wife, Shelley.

Bay, like her brother, is intense, outspoken, and incredibly gifted. During the first Reagan administration she served as treasurer of the United States—at thirty-two, the youngest in history. She manages her own political consultancy firm and has run for high public office herself—losing a bid to become California's state treasurer. As might be expected, she shares the Buchanan penchant for absolute loyalty. But she also is very independent and strong-willed.

It was Bay who finally convinced her brother to run against a weak, waffling, and wavering George Bush in 1992. His breach of the "no new taxes" pledge—as well as his subterfuge in funding abortion and homosexual groups—made him intolerable to the old Reagan conservative coalition. After Buchanan gave the incumbent the scare of his life in New Hampshire, a lack of money and a hostile press made the challenge untenable.

Though he played a major part in the convention that summer, once again he turned his attention to his journalistic career. But it was to be a short respite.

In 1996, Bay needed to do little persuading to get Buchanan in the race. Besides the fact that the Republicans were offering an extraordinarily weak field, his wife was urging him to run.

The former Shelley Scarney may actually have logged

more time on campaigns than her husband has. She was one of Richard Nixon's pool of secretaries and traveled with both the 1960 and 1968 campaigns. She and Buchanan met in New York when they both worked in Nixon's law office. In 1969, she became the presidential gatekeeper. They were married in 1971 with the president and first lady in attendance. By all accounts, she has a keen political mind—and though she craves privacy, she is a fierce competitor.

Thus, still surrounded by family, Pat Buchanan has entered into another fated campaign. Fighting and scraping with the world once again, he remains very much a man bound by the covenant of hearth and home.

We moderns hold to a strangely disjunctive view of the relationship between life and work—thus enabling us to nonchalantly separate a person's private character from his or her public accomplishments. But this novel divorce of root from fruit, however genteel, is a ribald denial of one of the most basic truths in life: What you are begets what you do; wrong-headed philosophies stem from wrong-headed philosophers; sin doesn't just happen—it is sinners that sin.

Thus, according to the English historian and journalist Hilaire Belloc, "Biography always affords the greatest insights into sociology. To comprehend the history of a thing is to unlock the mysteries of its present, and more, to discover the profundities of its future."[15] Similarly, the inimitable Samuel Johnson quipped,

Almost all the miseries of life, almost all the wickedness that infects society, and almost all the distresses that afflict mankind, are the consequences of some defect in private duties. Likewise, all the joys of this world may be attributable to the happiness of hearth and home.[16]

Or, as E. Michael Jones has asserted, "Biography is destiny."[17]

If that is true, then the remarkable biography of Pat Buchanan—one that has essentially been driven by the bonds of his relationships rather than the prods of his ambitions—offers a substantial clue to understanding his populist message.

PART II

Ideas Have Consequences

Progress has brought us both unbounded opportunities and unbridled difficulties. Thus, the measure of our civilization will not be that we have done much, but what we have done with that much. I believe that the next half century will determine if we will advance the cause of Christian civilization or revert to the horrors of brutal paganism. The thought of modern industry in the hands of Christian charity is a dream worth dreaming. The thought of industry in the hands of paganism is a nightmare beyond imagining. The choice between the two is upon us.

—*Theodore Roosevelt*[1]

CHAPTER 3

The Muckrakers

Gross and reckless assaults on character, whether on the stump or in a newspaper, magazine, or book, create a morbid and vicious public sentiment, and at the same time act as a profound deterrent to able men of normal sensitiveness and tend to prevent them from entering the public service at any price.

—*Theodore Roosevelt*[2]

The media has been anything but subtle in the way it has displayed its ferocious animosity to Patrick Buchanan's populist campaign. The headlines have screeched their disapproval with scowling adjectives and howling invectives.

Newsweek magazine ran a cover story with a banner that read, "Preaching fear: the world he's selling is stark and certain, a safe place for ordinary Americans worried about jobs and family. But Pat Buchanan's appeal is built on fear, and his raw campaign is troubling the party he hopes to lead."[3]

Time magazine's cover story bore the headline, "The case against Buchanan." A sidebar was emblazoned,

"Stinking to high heaven: why the rhetoric of people like Pat Buchanan gives America a bad odor."[4]

U.S. News and World Report offered readers a cover story bearing the slug-line, "The loose Buchanan: the GOP's panic attack." It was accompanied by an explanatory blurb that read, "Summoning angry voters to ride to the sound of the guns, he transforms the 1996 race."[5]

Again and again, Buchanan has been demonized by the media as an "unabashed hate-monger," a "homophobic, anti-Semitic, and woman-hating extremist," a "right-wing demagogue," and a "fringe public figure who is, for all intents and purposes, indistinguishable from David Duke."[6]

A survey of more than two hundred published articles in magazines, newspapers, and periodicals since the New Hampshire primary revealed that only twenty-two mentioned the substantive issue components of Buchanan's populist message, only nineteen quoted campaign supporters or workers at length, and a mere nine conveyed any positive connotations whatsoever.[7]

According to syndicated columnist Joe Sobran: "It is a tribute to Buchanan's force of personality that so few people can disagree with him in measured terms. Those who oppose him feel he has to be stopped, not refuted. They typically deal with him not in arguments, but in accusations."[8]

That is bias by any other name.

The Bias Cliché

There is only one thing a person can say in this day of brash intemperance that requires real courage—and that is a truism. A truism is often so biting and precise that it is discomfiting. It is anathema and thus scorned.

Making the accusation of media bias is a perfect case in point. Like a truism, it is universally acknowledged. And like anathema, it is simultaneously universally scorned. Even so, as is the case with most truisms, it is true.

After a comprehensive analysis of American network news coverage, conservative media pioneer Marlin Maddoux was forced to conclude:

> There wasn't a nickel's worth of difference among the *Big Three*—ABC, CBS, and NBC. The stories were basically the same; the bias in their coverage was the same. It became frighteningly clear that the television screen was dominated by the radical left. And opposing views were virtually closed out.[9]

Similarly, former Carter administration speech writer Philip Terzian was forced to acknowledge:

> For the most part, journalistic bias in favor of liberal causes and candidates is so obvious, so pervasive, so natural to the press corps, that it is scarcely worth noticing. There is a good reason why journalists react so churlishly to the charge: the evidence is so graphic.[10]

He is right. Most reporters do indeed deny any possibility of the taint of political bias—even when presented with the dumb certainties of evidence. They persist in maintaining airs of complete objectivity. Loudly and insistently.

New York Post reporter Bill Kantor lashed out that charges of a distinct liberal bias in the news were just "right-wing sour grapes."[11] Lisa McClellan, a Fox network producer, said that such criticisms were "ridiculous" and just "further proof of the right's obsession with conspiracy—more scary neo-fascist hysteria."[12] Mark Lowrey, a liberal syndicated columnist, asserted that:

> The far-right has always had a love-hate relationship with the press: they love to hate us. That is probably due to two different factors: first they can't bear to face the truth about the world, and second, they just don't know how to accept defeat at the ballot box. On both counts they feel compelled to find a scapegoat. Well, they're gonna have to find another goat to scape.[13]

U.S. News and World Report editor Harrison Rainie, unnerved by the charge of bias, responded: "That's crazy! The press has been, if anything, much more vigilant about fairness and objectivity and sort of explaining issues front to back than it ever has before."[14]

There are, of course, a few honest souls among the media mavens. Robert Bazell of NBC asserts that, "Objectivity is a fallacy. Journalism is almost always about a point of view."[15] Independent producer Linda Ellerbee agrees: "We report news, not truth. There is no such thing as objectivity. Any reporter who tells you he's objective is lying to you."[16] And Geraldo Rivera has argued—as well he might—that objectivity "was invented by journalism schools. It has very little to do with real life."[17]

For the most part, though, media spokesmen remain recalcitrant. Thus, Sam Donaldson has argued that: "The preponderance of the political press corps is very professional and objective. Our own political preferences rarely ever intrude. We just call 'em as we see 'em."[18]

Presuppositions

But of course that is precisely the problem. They "see 'em" through the very peculiar lens of a very particular worldview. Tom Brokaw quipped that "Bias, like beauty, is in the eye of the beholder."[19] Quite so. It is rooted in his or her unique vision of things.

And for the most part, that vision favors, for the most part, the left eye. Even if the famous Rothman-Lichter had not told us that more than 90 percent of newsmen today considered themselves "politically liberal," we might have guessed it—after all, if it looks like a duck, walks like a duck, and quacks like a duck, it is probably a duck.[20]

Of course, one look at the background of those covering the political scene indicates why. They are partisan liberals.

Jeff Gralnick, vice president and executive producer for ABC News, served as George McGovern's press secretary in 1972.[21] Jeff Greenfield, a leading political reporter for that network was a speech writer for Robert Kennedy in 1968.[22]

Dotty Lynch, the political editor for CBS was employed by the Democratic National Committee for two years and later served both the Gary Hart and the Walter Mondale campaigns as a pollster in 1984.[23]

Tom Johnson, the president of CNN, was Lyndon Johnson's deputy press secretary and later became a special assistant in the Johnson White House.[24] Ken Bode, a political correspondent for the network, was an aide to Morris Udall in 1976 and drafted the 1972 McGovern Commission Democratic delegate reform rules.[25]

John Chancellor, the recently retired special editorial commentator for NBC, served in the Kennedy and Johnson Administrations.[26] Tim Russert, vice president of NBC News and the Washington bureau chief, served as chief of staff to Senator Daniel Patrick Moynihan and as a counselor to Mario Cuomo.[27] And Maria Shriver, a reporter and producer for the network, worked in the McGovern campaign in 1972 as well as the Kennedy campaign in 1980.[28]

National Public Radio president Douglas Bennet served in the Carter administration and worked in the senate offices of both Tom Eagleton and Abraham Ribicoff.[29] Bob Ferrante, the executive producer of morning news, was the director of communications for the Democratic National Committee for two years.[30] Anne Edwards, a senior editor for radio news, served the Mondale campaign as a scheduler.[31]

Kwame Holman worked as Mayor Marion Barry's press secretary before coming to the *PBS Newshour* as a lead political reporter.[32]

Time's deputy Washington bureau chief, Margaret Carlson, served in the Carter administration, as did Walter Shapiro, a senior political writer for the magazine.[33]

Kathryn Bushkin, the director of editorial administration for *U.S. News and World Report,* was Gary Hart's press secretary in 1984.[34] Harrison Rainie, the magazine's assistant managing editor, was the chief of staff to Senator Daniel Patrick Moynihan.[35]

And so the story goes. At every major media outlet in America, key positions are filled with political and ideological partisans of the left. That being the case, the only thing really surprising about the press coverage of the current political scene is that it is not *even more biased* than it has been.

Thus, as Neil Postman and Steve Powers assert in their remarkable book *How to Watch TV News,* "Every news story is a reflection of the reporter who tells the story."[36]

Herbert Gans, a renowned media analyst, has said:

Journalism is, like sociology, an empirical discipline. As a result, the news consists not only of the findings of an inquiry, but also of the concepts and methods which go into that inquiry, the assumptions that underlie those concepts and methods, and even a further set of assumptions, which could in turn be tested—if only journalists had the time.[37]

Those assumptions and presuppositions ultimately drive what is and what is not revealed in, by, and through the media. Again, according to Postman and Powers:

> Most news does not inhere in the event. An event *be-comes* news. And it becomes news because it is selected for notice out of the buzzing, booming confusion around us. This may seem a fairly obvious point but keep in mind that many people believe that the news is always *out there,* waiting to be gathered or collected. In fact, the news is more often *made* rather than gathered. And it is made on the basis of what the journalist *thinks* is impor-tant or what the journalist thinks the audience *thinks* is important.[38]

Therefore, they say, "a viewer must know something about the political beliefs and economic situation of those who provide the news."[39] It is, after all, not the world *as it is* that they present day after day in their reports, columns, stories, and broadcasts; it is the world *as they believe it is*—or even, *as they believe it ought to be.*

Lincoln Steffens, a journalist working during the early part of this century, proved that he could "create a crime wave" anytime he wanted simply by writing about all the criminal activity that normally occurs in the New York metropolitan region during any given month. He could then "end the crime wave" simply by not tallying the lists of crimes committed.[40]

Cecil Chesterton and A. R. Orage, English journalists of the same era, conducted a similar exercise in London. They created a scandalous hysteria simply by reporting all the odd doings of Parliament members in and around Westminster.[41]

In both cases, journalists were able to transform public perceptions, not by manufacturing events, but by highlighting generally neglected facts about the actual everyday affairs of modern urban life. They were able to change the course of future events by giving their own peculiar slant to prior events.

Evidence of the power of the media to shape public opinion is not just anecdotal. Virtually every American demographic and sociological study over the past thirty years has underscored the tremendous impact that newspapers, television, radio, magazines, and other popular mediums have on the way we think, feel, and behave.[42] More often than not, the perception of the world that the man on the street has is shaped by what journalists *choose to emphasize* as opposed to what they *choose not to emphasize*.[43]

Philosopher Francis Schaeffer pointed out this fact in his seminal work *How Should We Then Live?* He wrote: "There are certain news organizations, newspapers, news magazines, wire services, and news broadcasts which have the ability to generate news. They are the news-makers, and when an item appears in them, it becomes news. When it is omitted, it is not news."[44]

Only God controls events. But the media controls what we know of those events—or even *whether* we know of them. They are indeed the news-makers.

News-Makers

The literary lion Sidney Lanier once commented that "small minds love to bring large news, and failing a load, will make one."[45] What was once merely epigrammatic is now epidemic.

Historian Daniel Boorstin observes that there was once a time when journalists saw their task simply in terms of recording events—precisely as they occurred. They believed that "the responsibility for making news was entirely God's—or the Devil's. The newsman's task was only to give an account of such considerable things as arrived unto their notice."[46]

Thus, James Parton observed in 1866, "The skilled and faithful journalist recording with exactness and power the thing that has come to pass, is Providence addressing men."[47] Similarly, Charles Dana, the great nineteenth-century editor of the New York *Sun*, declared, "I have always felt that whatever Divine Providence permitted to occur, I was not too proud to report."[48] Or as Joe Friday was wont to say, "The facts ma'am. Just the facts."[49]

Of course, this notion no longer has much currency. If our daily newspaper is boring, we are likely to blame the reporter, whereas our ancestors would have blamed the day. As Boorstin has commented: "We need not be theologians to see that we have shifted responsibility for making the world interesting from God to the newspaperman."[50]

Thus, no longer content to be news-gatherers, journalists have become instead, news-makers. No longer satisfied with merely reporting the news, they look for the "story behind the event." They want to convey more than news; they desire to be purveyors of *truth*.

A generation ago, the great writer and editor Walter Lippman offered a clear warning against that kind of aspiration. He said: "The function of *news* is to signalize an event; the function of *truth* is to bring to light the hidden facts, to set them in relation with each other, and make a picture of reality on which men can act."[51]

According to Lippman, the dramatic distinction between the *news* and *truth* stems not solely from the inadequacies of journalists, but also "from the exigencies of the news business, which limits the time, space, and resources that can be allotted to any single story."[52]

He argued that if the public required "a more truthful interpretation of the world" they lived in, they would have to "depend on institutions other than the press."[53] Postman and Powers concur, saying, "Anyone who relies exclusively on the news for his or her knowledge of the world is making a serious mistake."[54]

Schaeffer comments:

Many viewers seem to assume that when they have seen something on TV, they have seen it with their own eyes. It makes the viewer think he has actually been on the

scene. He knows, because his own eyes have seen. He has
the impression of greater direct objective knowledge
than ever before. For many, what they see on television
becomes more true than what they see with their eyes in
the external world. But this is not so, for one must never
forget that every television minute has been edited. The
viewer does not see the event. He sees an edited form of
the event. It is not the event which is seen, but an edited
symbol or an edited image of the event. An aura and
illusion of objectivity and truth is built up, which could
not be totally the case if the people shooting the film
were completely neutral. The physical limitations of the
camera dictate that only one aspect of the total situation
is given. If the camera were aimed ten feet to the left or
ten feet to the right, an entirely different *objective story*
might come across. And on top of that, the people taking
the film and editing it often do have a subjective view-
point that enters in. When we see a political figure on
TV, we are not seeing the person as he necessarily is; we
are seeing, rather, the image someone has decided we
should see.[55]

In the ideological and commercial world of media,
presuppositional worldviews will skew the product
toward a particular perspective and away from another.
That is simply the order of things in this poor fallen
world.

The Houston Myth

At the 1992 Republican National Convention in the Houston Astrodome, Pat Buchanan made a barn-burner of a speech that highlighted all of the themes he would later make the centerpiece of his populist campaign. In it, he was both unrelenting and prophetic about the controversial Democratic nominee and his even more controversial wife:

> The agenda Clinton and Clinton would impose on America—abortion on demand, a litmus test for the Supreme Court, homosexual rights, discrimination against religious schools, women in combat—that's change all right. But it is not the kind of change America wants. It is not the kind of change America needs. And it is not the kind of change we can tolerate in a nation we still call God's country.[56]

He continued: "There is a religious war going on in this country for the soul of America. It is a Cultural War, as critical to the kind of nation we shall one day be—as was the Cold War itself."[57]

It has become a matter of common wisdom political orthodoxy that Buchanan "probably fatally wounded any chances George Bush had for re-election that evening."[58] In fact, our collective memory has been colored by the notion that the speech was "delivered with a zeal that appalled most of his listeners" and "alienated the nation from his party."[59]

In fact, the speech did nothing of the kind. Immediately following the speech, John Chancellor commented, "I thought it was an excellent speech. It was an amazing speech in a hall this size. I think it shows the party coming together. I think Pat really helped them."[60]

Several other convention veterans agreed. According to David Brinkley, "It was an outstandingly good speech."[61] Cokie Roberts said, "This hit all of the themes that go to Reagan Democrats—the question of abortion, of gay rights, of the environment seeming a little cockeyed."[62]

"I've covered seventeen national conventions," Hal Bruno of ABC said, "and I've never seen a better first night."[63]

"Viewed in terms of classic raw rhetoric," said Sander Vanocur, the Buchanan speech "was the most skillful attempt to remind the party faithful of the role that ideas have played in American politics since Eugene McCarthy nominated Adlai Stevenson at the 1960 Democratic Convention."[64]

Listening with one of the state delegations on the floor, Ted Koppel observed, "They walked out of here tonight enthusiastic, they walked out of here with something that Republicans have not had for quite a few months, a sense of optimism." He concluded, "Our ABC poll, taken over the past five days, shows the gap narrowing to 20 points. By tomorrow, that gap will have appreciably narrowed. You can count on it."[65]

And, as it turned out, Koppel was right.

The overnight Hotline poll showed Bush soaring

from sixteen points down Monday, to six points down Tuesday—a ten-point leap in a single twenty-four-hour period, which ultimately proved to be the best day of the entire 1992 campaign.[66] Several other polls confirmed similar surges. For instance, the *New York Times–CBS* survey that had Clinton leading Bush by eighteen points just days before the Houston speech found Clinton just two points ahead, forty-eight to forty-six, the night afterward.[67]

Buchanan had succeeded in shifting the political agenda—from the economy, where 80 percent of the country thought America was "on the wrong track,"[68] to issues of morality and culture, apparently Clinton's weakest suits.

So, how did this roaring success come to be portrayed as a political and tactical disaster?

The follow-up media—perhaps realizing the *coup de grâce* that Buchanan had pulled off—began a full-scale attack on both the speech and the speaker. *USA Today* quipped that Buchanan had left Americans with "an intolerant image."[69] CBS reporter David Culhane murmured about his "rigid conceptions of family life and social issues."[70] On CNN Margaret Warner bemoaned his "appeal to bigotry and fear."[71] On *Today* Scott Simon complained of "a lack of tolerance, an incivility, and a lack of manners."[72] *Good Morning America* gave vent to Lance Morrow's opinion that he had given the proceedings an "ugly, narrow, and sectarian right-wing intolerance."[73]

Meanwhile, C-SPAN broadcast an Eleanor Clift diatribe against all of the delegates at the convention. Using a very broad anti-Buchanan brush, she condemned the attendees, who were, to her mind, "a group of the most intolerant human beings that could ever be collected."[74] Similarly, Linda Ellerbee brandished her preachments: "As you probably already know by now, the Republican platform was written by Miss Grundy, and if you're white enough, wealthy enough, and selfish enough, you, too, can be a Republican this year."[75]

Apparently, facts are of little consequence when it comes to reporting the news.

Prattfalls

The media's Milli Vanilli lip-synching of the liberal party line provides stark evidence that it has tossed any semblance of impartiality or objectivity to the four winds.

But that is not the most disturbing aspect of current political coverage. Bias is a fairly straightforward vice. What is even more insidious than an absence of factual objectivity is an absence of professional integrity—journalists have been ventriloquists instead of orators.

The essence of science is precision. The essence of sentiment is presumption. Because the media has difficulty distinguishing one from the other, it is both precise and presumptuous—but about exactly the wrong things. When it comes to coverage of Buchanan, the media has been very scientific about sentimental things, but very sentimental about scientific things.

They have, in short, not checked the facts, not verified the data, and not understood the issues at hand. They have invariably taken the easy way out—by retrofitting news releases from liberal lobbyists and publicists and simply adding their byline.

Instead of working harder, they shouted louder. Instead of striving for professional excellence, they have settled for professional expediency. Instead of attempting to grasp their subject matter, they have grasped at straws—and straw men.

The flap over Larry Pratt, a Buchanan campaign aid, is a case in point.

Just days before the critical New Hampshire primary, the Center for Public Integrity—a decidedly left-wing lobbying group in Washington—released a report linking Pratt with a number of unsavory militia, anti-Semitic, and white supremacist groups.[76]

Almost immediately, virtually every major media outlet in the nation accepted the story uncritically and broadcast it for full effect. It was the lead story for nearly two full days—an eternity in a political campaign.

In fact, the story was entirely fabricated.

Pratt is an elder in a racially mixed evangelical Presbyterian church. One of his pastors is black. He has been married for more than thirty years to a Latin American—and they speak Spanish in their home. He is a member of the Congress of Racial Equality and of Jews for the Preservation of Firearms Ownership. He has been publicly active and vocal in the issues of racial reconciliation, crime and justice, and social cohesion.

To accuse Larry Pratt of racism or anti-Semitism is either the height of ignorance or the height of impudence. That kind of dull dishonesty is either a sign of faulty discipline or faulty ethics. Or maybe both.

Calumny

It is often said that a picture is worth a thousand words. But, according to Postman and Powers, "it is probably equally true that one word is worth a thousand pictures, at least sometimes—for example, when it comes to understanding the world we live in."[77] They say: "The whole problem with the news comes down to this: all the words uttered in an hour of news coverage could be printed on a single page. And the world cannot be understood in one page."[78]

But besides these rather understandable limits of time and space, there are moral limits as well. According to the veteran journalist Jimmy Breslin, today's media moguls are the heirs of a rather steadily eroding moral tradition. He says that news organizations all too often succumb to "bribery, extortion, calumny, also known as slander, and two kinds of lies, bald-faced and by omission."[79] For some this causes more than a little confusion because, after all, "the sins being committed at typewriters are greater than the ones being written about."[80] In fact, Breslin says, "there is no situation so bad that a fresh edition of the morning newspaper can't make worse."[81]

Because liberal journalists so heartily abhor his populist message, Pat Buchanan has become a particular target of their selective and wrathful reportage. They have thus emphasized rhetoric over reality. They have highlighted image over substance. With a don't-confuse-me-with-the-facts passion to replace ideals that are universal with ideas that are miscellaneous, they have remade the political ecology after their own fallen likeness—which has always been the primordial impulse of sin.

Clearly, the media's smothering uniformity of purpose is less a horrifying conspiracy than it is a harmonic convergence—though the results would surely have been about the same either way. Perhaps it was this very kind of perverse calumny that provoked H. L. Mencken, the profound pundit of the last generation, to comment bitterly that:

> All the durable truths that have come into the world within historic times have been opposed as bitterly as if they were so many waves of small pox, and every individual who has welcomed and advocated them, absolutely, without exception, has been denounced and punished as an enemy of the race. In that kind of atmosphere, with that kind of publicity, the connoisseur of the higher political mountebankery cannot fail to gain the upper hand.[82]

If that be the case, may we be ever vigilant to rectify the situation—lest our republic be torn asunder by the bacchic asceticism of the day.[83] Today, it is Pat Buchanan and his grass-roots political campaign, tomorrow it may be you—or me.

CHAPTER 4

Pat Answers

No abounding of material prosperity shall avail us if our spiritual senses atrophy. The foes of our own household will surely prevail against us unless there be in our people an inner life which finds its outer expression in a morality like unto that preached by the seers and prophets of God when the grandeur that was Greece and the glory that was Rome still lay in the future.

—*Theodore Roosevelt*[1]

Patrick Buchanan, who as a protest candidate ran unsuccessfully for the 1992 nomination against President George Bush, was widely expected this time around to vanish in a field jammed with seemingly like-minded conservatives.

Instead, he has mixed his calls for tax cuts and his bedrock social conservatism with an unabashed economic nationalism that is not just rattling the current political ecology. With his dire warnings of an ever-encroaching "new world order," he is widening post–Cold War cracks among Main Street and Wall Street Republicans over foreign and economic policy.

At a time when sound bytes and photo-ops seem to

dominate our political discourse, Buchanan has done the unthinkable: He has run an issues campaign. He has addressed the plaguing questions of our time directly and substantively. Even those who strongly disagree with some of the positions he ultimately takes—and many of his strongest supporters do in one area or another—must give him grudging respect on this ground. He is not afraid to take a stand.

Although he has not been shy about staking out and defending controversial positions, three issues have brought him under particular scrutiny. And though the various media outlets have raised a considerable hullabaloo over them, they have only offered viewers and readers cursory shorthand versions of his actual statements on anti-Semitism, economic nationalism, and modern moral issues.

Thus Buchanan's own words prove to be more than a little instructive.

Anti-Semitism

Buchanan has continually repudiated the ideas, symbols, advocates, and insinuations of anti-Semitism. He has never wavered on this issue—nor has he ever given the impression in his personal or his public life that he harbors any latent temptations to do so. He has said:

No true Christian can carry within his heart hatred for any of God's children. I am as aware as any other Christian that our Savior was Jewish. His mother was Jewish.

The Apostles were Jewish. The first martyrs were Jewish. So no true Christian, in my judgment, can be an anti-Semite.[2]

Indeed, *Time* magazine has confirmed that "Buchanan has condemned anti-Semitism, once even comparing it to pornography."[3]

Apparently this is not enough to convince some of his political opponents. Nearly every article written and every story broadcast about him somehow manages to repeat charges that he is secretly an anti-Semite. Not only do such charges fly in the face of his very clear and unequivocal testimony, they contradict a very public record over the course of some twenty years in the public eye.

In fact, the charges are based on political disputes—provoked in part by stands that Buchanan has taken over the years that have angered some columnists, lobbyists, and pundits. They are rooted, in part, in disagreements about the direction of American foreign policy and have nothing to do with supposed expressions of racist sentiment.

Interestingly, Buchanan has always favored a strong, independent state of Israel. He has been a lifelong friend to the Jewish people, both individually and collectively speaking. In 1973, as a special assistant to President Nixon, he enthusiastically supported the decision to aid the Israelis with a massive airlift that ultimately saved the country during the dire days of the Yom Kippur War.

In 1976, he supported the Israeli raid on Entebbe, and in 1981 he supported the Begin government's stealth attack on Iraq's fledgling nuclear reactor program.

In 1986, he was instrumental in securing the release of Natan Sharanski from the Soviet Gulag—working closely with his wife, Avital.

His newspaper columns throughout his twenty years as a syndicated writer contain numerous affirmations of his view that the U.S. has a "moral commitment to guarantee the security and survival of the Israeli state."[4]

But while he has been a defender of Israel, he has not been an uncritical defender.

He has, for instance, advocated the "land for peace" policy in the Middle East. Though now the official policy of the Israeli government, this has rankled the ire of many hard-core supporters of uncompromised Herzelian Zionism.

Though he favored deterring Saddam Hussein's aggression in Saudi Arabia, he also questioned the wisdom of the American commitment to reestablish the Emir of Kuwait following the Iraqi takeover of the Persian Gulf region—because he feared it would put American lives at stake in a conflict that was not clearly in the nation's vital interest.

He also publicly defended John Demjanjuk, a retired Cleveland auto worker, against the charge that he was "Ivan the Terrible," a Treblinka death camp guard responsible for the heinous mass murder of Jews during the Second World War. Despite deportation by the U.S. Justice Department on the basis of evidence falsified by the Soviet KGB, the Israeli Supreme Court subsequently ruled that Demjanjuk was a victim of mistaken identity—a fact that Buchanan had maintained all along.

Each of these policies and positions has been cited as evidence that Buchanan is a racist and an anti-Semite. In addition, several anecdotal stories have also been circulated to further prove the point.

It has been widely reported, for instance, that Buchanan told Elie Wiesel that President Reagan must not surrender to "Jewish pressure" against visiting a German cemetery where a number of notorious Nazis were buried. The story was originally broadcast on NBC by Marvin Kalb, just before President Reagan made a controversial visit to Bitburg cemetery in 1985. Kalb reported that Buchanan had been observed writing, "over and over again: succumbing to the pressure of the Jews." The alleged source of the story later told the *New York Times* that Kalb was entirely mistaken about the notation, and that "this is a complete flap over nothing." Any criticism of Buchanan, he said, "is a bum rap." Kalb later apologized for the report. Nevertheless it still circulates.[5]

Another widely circulated story involves a 1977 column in which Buchanan called Hitler an "individual of great courage" who possessed "extraordinary gifts."[6] In the reports, the excerpted phrases from the column are intended to leave the impression that the column was a tribute to Adolf Hitler. In reality, the column was, in large part, an account of historian John Toland's widely acclaimed biography of Hitler. Buchanan merely summarized Toland's depiction of Hitler:

Though Hitler was indeed racist and anti-Semitic to the core, a man who without compunction could commit murder and genocide, he was also an individual of great courage, a soldier's soldier in the Great War, a political organizer of the first rank, a leader steeped in the history of Europe, who possessed oratorical powers that could awe even those who despised him.[7]

In the same column Buchanan wrote that "Hitler was marching along the road toward a New Order where Western civilization would not survive." Far from an endorsement of the Fascist dictator, the column warned of making the same mistake with Mao Tse-Tung and Taiwan in 1977 that deluded Western leaders made with Hitler and Czechoslovakia in the 1930s.[8]

In an interview in *Present Tense* magazine, Buchanan stated:

"If my friends in the Jewish community feel Pat Buchanan, a traditionalist Catholic, owes some kind of apology for the record of the Holy Father during World War II, they can wait, because it's not going to be forthcoming."[9] The context of the comment was the demand by Bronx Rabbi Avraham Weiss for the Catholic Church to expel Carmelite nuns from their convent at Auschwitz, on the grounds that their presence there was an insult to Jewish sensibilities, since Pope Pius XII and the church were allegedly complicit in the Holocaust. Weiss actually invaded the convent at Auschwitz to protest the nuns' presence.[10] The *Boston Herald* wrote in defense of Weiss's actions, saying: "The coldness of it was numb-

ing: On the spot where one-quarter of European Jewry
was martyred, the church that for 1,000 years had done
so much to feed anti-Semitism intended to set up
shop."[11]

Buchanan went on to write a column defending the
Catholic Church and Pope Pius XII against the slur—
which had its origins in Rolf Hochhuth's fictional play
The Deputy[12] in 1963—and pointing out that the contemporary testimony of Jewish leaders contradicted the
charges. In fact it actually praised Pius XII for saving
Jewish lives.[13]

Even Buchanan's fiercest critics and most vociferous
accusers admit that all these supposed instances of supposed anti-Semitic statements and incidents hardly make
a sound case—even when taken together.[14] But their
suspicions seemed confirmed by a statement he made
off-the-cuff one evening in 1990. Appearing on television's discussion format program, *The McLaughlin Report*, Buchanan argued against a hasty involvement in
the Persian Gulf War with Saddam Hussein, saying:
"There are only two groups that are beating the drums
for war in the middle East, the Israeli Defense Ministry
and its amen corner in the United States."[15]

The context in which Buchanan spoke reveals his rea-
sons for speaking. Early in the Gulf crisis, before the
massive buildup of American and Allied ground troops
in the Gulf, some columnists in the U.S. and a number
of Israeli officials were clamoring for an early preemptive
strike against Iraq. According to one account in the *New*

York Times: "Many Israeli politicians, academic experts and citizens are growing nervous, and in some cases angry, after concluding that the United States wants a political solution and is not looking for a military confrontation in the Persian Gulf."[16]

Prime Minister Shamir's chief of staff even went so far as to assert, "If the United States doesn't solve the problem now then, they'll have to fly the Marines back here again."[17] Many military experts agreed that such unilateral action would risk a disaster.

It was in this context that Buchanan made his now infamous remark. Interestingly, it was more than a month later that a columnist from the *New York Times,* A. M. Rosenthal, dusted off that old footage and made the first public accusation of anti-Semitism against Buchanan.[18]

According to the influential publisher of *Commentary* magazine, Norman Podhoretz, the offhand comment represented "the classically anti-Semitic canard of dual loyalty."[19] That single remark alone, he argued, "settled the issue of Buchanan's anti-Semitism" for him.[20]

But it hardly settled the issue for those who knew Buchanan best. Michael Kinsley, Buchanan's ideological sparring partner on CNN's *Crossfire* said: "As a Jew, I never felt any hostility from Buchanan on that score— never heard him make a disparaging remark about Jews, never noticed any difference in the way he treats Jews and non-Jews."[21]

According to another colleague, syndicated columnist Robert Novak:

Even after the Rosenthal column, nobody responsible in the Republican Party said, "Yes, Pat Buchanan is an anti-Semite." They didn't join in. Very few journalists joined in. What happened was, when he entered presidential politics, then he entered a new level of criticism and attack on him.[22]

Jack Germond of the *Baltimore Sun* concurred, saying:

I've known Pat Buchanan now for twenty-five years. We have agreed on almost nothing, starting with Richard Nixon. But there's not a scintilla of evidence in all I've known about Pat that he is anti-Semitic. This is an attempt to say that if you disagree with Israel on a matter of policy, you can be called anti-Semitic.[23]

Recently, Bruce Herschensohn penned an article in the *Los Angeles Times* entitled, "The Man I Know Isn't a Racist." He wrote: "It is not my habit to start articles by stating my religion or declaring a personal friendship, but under today's conditions, it is vital. I'm Jewish and Pat Buchanan is my friend."[24]

Herschensohn, a former Los Angeles television commentator and Republican senatorial candidate, is currently a fellow at the John F. Kennedy School of Government Institute of Politics at Harvard. He continued:

I have no problem with anyone being critical of him on any number of issues, but I am infuriated, enraged, and incensed at the attacks that have labeled him an anti-

Semite and a racist. I remember when Pat passionately wanted to risk a superpower confrontation to prevent the possible destruction of Israel as the Yom Kippur War started in 1973. He forcefully condemned the ACLU for its 1978 support of Nazis marching in Skokie, Illinois. Although there were "inside" political risks, he opposed the Reagan Administration's condemnation of Israel in 1981 when Israel bombed Iraq's nuclear reactor. I can say without hesitancy that from what I know about Pat, which is a great deal, the charges I have heard against him have absolutely no credibility, but they are very dangerous.[25]

Though clearly politically motivated, the slanderous accusations against Buchanan, Herschensohn argued, had far greater implications than merely the ruination of a single candidate:

In the attempt to destroy his candidacy for the presidency, such slander not only puts Pat Buchanan on the defensive—which is the objective—it also puts millions of his supporters on the defensive, and in their passion for him, some of them may transfer their anger against his critics to anger against the groups that Pat is accused of hating. Moreover, these charges are putting the United States, as a nation, on the defensive. Just after the New Hampshire primary, a foreign correspondent asked me, "How can an anti-Semite and a racist get so far in presidential politics in these times?" I answered that someone so described cannot get very far in U.S. presidential politics. Immediately he told me that he was talking about

Pat Buchanan. Immediately I told him he was severely misinformed. But foreign correspondents can send untruths just as easily as facts beyond our water's edge.[26]

Indeed they can. For instance, Israel's largest newspaper, *Yediot Aharonot*, editorialized, "Will a man who hates Jews and blacks represent the Republican Party in the race for the White House?" Spain's *El Pais* newspaper wrote that Buchanan's declarations are always tinged with "racism and anti-Semitism." Frankfurt's *Allgemeine Zeltung* alleged that "the American presidential campaign now has its own Zhirinovsky."[27]

Sadly, such outrageous comments generally go unchallenged in this day of rumor and innuendo.

Economic Nationalism

Charges of isolationism and protectionism have brought Buchanan nearly as much heated invective as has the charge of anti-Semitism. According to Buchanan, once a staunch "free trade" advocate, his relatively new commitment to "fair trade" is based upon two fundamental conservative principles.

The first fundamental principle is political nationalism. Buchanan declares that international agreements such as the North American Free Trade Agreement (NAFTA), the General Agreement on Tariffs and Trade (GATT), and the infamous bailout of the Mexican peso have resulted in the continued surrender of American sovereignty to the institutions of the new world order—an

order defined and administered by the bureaucratic minions of such global cartels as the World Trade Organization, the Trilateral Commission, the Council on Foreign
Relations, and the United Nations.

The second fundamental principle upon which his
populist trade platform is built is economic nationalism.
Buchanan says the new global trade agreements are cost-
ing U.S. workers jobs. It is immoral, he asserts, to force
American textile workers who make nine dollars an hour
to compete with Chinese workers who make twenty-five
cents an hour. But that is a fact very few in the political
apparatus seem to want to talk about. Thus, he claims,
neither party in Washington seems to be too terribly
concerned about the ordinary working people of this
country.

As a corrective, Buchanan would impose reactive tariffs on some of the nation's biggest trading partners—
particularly Japan, which he has accused of having
targeted American industries no less effectively than they
targeted Pearl Harbor at the beginning of the Second
World War.

That kind of a message can be rather disconcerting
and disorienting to mainstream Republicans who have in
recent years become accustomed to hearing their political leaders extol the virtues of free trade.

But Buchanan is unflinching in his populist message.
He has even gone so far as to say:

There is no doubt there is an inherent contradiction between conservatism and unfettered capitalism. Conserva-

tives ought to be worshiping at a higher altar than the bottom line on a balance sheet. What in heaven's name is it that we conservatives want to conserve if not social stability and family unity?[28]

Because of such ideas, many establishment Republicans have branded Buchanan a turncoat. The neo-conservative magazine, *Weekly Standard,* for instance, trumpeted the charge that Buchanan was "America's last leftist." The scathing article declared, "Buchanan has moved to the left of President Clinton. He has turned his back on the fundamental convictions that have defined American conservatism for 40 years."[29]

Buchanan responds with a flurry of facts and figures:

This year the U.S. merchandise trade deficit is running at $200 billion. By Trade Representative Mickey Kantor's own figures—$1 billion in exports equals 20,000 jobs— our appetite for foreign goods will cost fellow Americans four million jobs. One wonders what it takes to shake our free-trade friends out of their dogmatic slumber.[30]

He argues that since the Nixon era, the dollar has fallen 75 percent against the yen, 60 percent against the mark. In 1950 America produced half the world's goods. Today, our workers produce less than a fourth. And for the first time, more Americans work in government than in manufacturing.[31]

And that may not be the worst of it, he says:

We pay in other coin, too, for worshiping this golden calf: in lost sovereignty, as we implore a powerful new World Trade Organization to let us defend crucial U.S. interests; in a growing dependency on foreigners to buy our bonds and sell us their oil; in $50 billion bailouts of bankrupts like Mexico, lest they collapse and take us down with them. We are paying, too, in social costs: in a burnt-out Detroit, once the forge of the Great Arsenal of Democracy; in ghost towns that were once factory towns; in the stagnant wages of an alienated working class and a middle class newly introduced to insecurity.[32]

His arguments are compelling and shaped by his many years of political pragmatism:

If Republicans cannot see the economic consequences of this New World Order, they had best recognize the political. In 1992 a third of the Reagan coalition bolted to Ross Perot. By the time the NAFTA passed, grass-roots Republicans had turned against it. GATT had to be rammed through a lame-duck session of Congress. To ship Mexico tens of billions to pay off its bondholders at Citibank and Goldman Sachs, President Clinton had to act by executive order. You don't need a weatherman to know which way the wind is blowing. But why do Republicans remain fixated on "free-trade" ideology?[33]

Not untypically, Buchanan's appeal is based on more than political pragmatism. It is rooted in a profound grasp of American history and the great conservative traditions of the Republican Party of yore:

Woodrow Wilson was our century's first free-trade president. But he was no conservative. Frederick Bastiat, French celebrant of free trade, declared as its end, "formation of a peaceful, ecumenical, indissoluble union of the peoples of the world." One understands why Deputy Secretary of State Strobe Talbott would buy into such nonsense. But why have U.S. conservatives become such zealous converts? The opportunity is at hand to jettison a New World Order Americans have rejected in their hearts, to build a new coalition of supply-siders and economic nationalists. Marry the growth agenda of Ronald Reagan to the America First philosophy of the four men whose faces are carved on Mount Rushmore—and the future is ours.[34]

His carefully constructed economic plan is designed to make America the enterprise zone of the industrial world once again. It begins with at least five key reforms to the current tax code.

First, impose a flat tax on incomes above $25,000 for a family of four with deductions only for mortgage interest and charitable contributions. By simplifying the tax code, he asserts, the government could radically downsize the IRS.[35]

Second, impose a flat tax on big corporations, with a much lower tax rate on small businesses. He argues that this would leave in the cash drawers of our job-creating small companies more income to hire American workers.[36]

Third, eliminate taxes on interest and dividends for individuals to spur family saving and investment. This provision, he says, would allow families to preserve their inheritance rather than lay up their treasures for nameless, faceless government bureaucrats.[37]

Fourth, eliminate inheritance taxes on family farms, businesses, and estates of less than $5 million. He says this would let children inherit what they, their parents, and grandparents put together with sweat and sacrifice.[38]

Fifth, declare a six-month holiday where long-term capital gains would be taxed at sales-tax rates. This would unlock hundreds of billions in assets, he says—stocks, bonds, real estate, equipment—and as a result, a volcano of activity would erupt.[39]

The message that this reformed U.S. tax code would send, he says, would be profound: "Work, save, invest here in the land of the free, and you will retain more of your earnings than in any other country."[40]

As this tax reform provides for some capital gains and estate tax revenue, Buchanan claims that such a flat tax rate can be lower than the oft-recommended 17 percent. And, he says, it could be lowered farther still by using revenue from consumption taxes on foreign goods.

Thus, Buchanan's program calls for several further reform measures.

First, impose a 10 percent tariff on Japanese imports. This would, he estimates, generate $12 billion—enough to eliminate almost all U.S. taxes on small business.[41]

Second, impose a 20 percent tariff on Chinese imports. China is using its $35 billion trade surplus with the U.S. to pursue policies of belligerence and repres-

sion. He argues therefore that we ought not accord it
the same privileged trade status we accord Britain. The
$8 billion this tariff would yield is enough to pay fully
for eliminating inheritance taxes on all U.S. small businesses and family farms.[42]

Third, impose a social tariff on Third World manufac-
tured goods. The purpose of this measure, Buchanan
says, is to insulate the wages of U.S. workers from down-
ward pressure from foreign laborers who must work for
$1 an hour or less. It is mindless, he asserts, to enact
health, safety, and environmental laws, wage laws and
family leave laws, and then, via NAFTA and GATT, to
invite the very companies Congress is regulating to
move to Mexico or Asia.[43]

He answers charges that a tariff on China or Japan will
make Iowa "a dust bowl" with yet another flurry of facts
and figures:

> Together, Japan and China enjoy a $100 billion trade
> surplus at our expense. Japan has 25 percent of the U.S.
> auto market; we have but 1 percent of Japan's. The Japa-
> nese economy is four times as dependent on sales to us as
> we are on sales to Japan. Would Tokyo toss this away out
> of pique at a trade hawk in the Oval Office? If foreign
> regimes don't like the new U.S. policy, let them not like
> it. This is our land; America is our country; the U.S. is
> our market. We decide who enters here and who does
> not. Toward free traders let us practice free trade. With
> predatory traders, it is time we learned to play hardball
> again. As for multinational-corporations, whose loyalty is

only to the bottom line on a balance sheet, inform these amoral behemoths they are welcome to bring in their capital and build their plants. But if they shut down factories here to open overseas, they will pay a price for the readmission of their goods into America's market. Who, after all, is the American economy for, if not Americans?[44]

This approach to economic issues, he contends, marries the growth ideas of Ronald Reagan to the "American System" devised by Alexander Hamilton and George Washington, pursued by Thomas Jefferson and Abraham Lincoln, and perfected by Theodore Roosevelt and Calvin Coolidge. Indeed, that system converted America from a seaboard country of farmers into the mightiest industrial power on earth.

Many Republicans, however, are not buying such ideas. They believe Pat Buchanan's views are un-Republican—and out of step with the great traditions of the party. On that point there has been almost unanimous consent from his rivals.

However, from a historical perspective, it is Buchanan who best exemplifies traditional Republican thinking on trade issues—not Bob Dole, Steve Forbes, Jack Kemp, or Bill Kristol. In fact, Buchanan's populist economic program merely pressed a venerable old hot button that had energized many nineteenth-century Republican campaigns. Thus, by blasting one-sided global trade deals that have cost thousands of American workers their jobs, he has actually reinvigorated the old economic nationalist tradition in the Republican Party.

According to Alfred Eckes, professor of history at Ohio University and a former chairman of the United States International Trade Commission, since the Second World War, the party establishment has embraced free trade and economic internationalism as a grand panacea for global problems. However, from a historical perspective, Buchanan best exemplifies traditional Republican thinking on trade issues. In a rather contrarian article in the *New York Times*, Eckes wrote:

> From Abraham Lincoln in 1860 to Alf Landon in 1936, every Republican presidential candidate ran on a platform endorsing high protective tariffs. A century ago, American politicians considered free trade an epithet and protectionism an accolade. Most Republican candidates proudly embraced economic nationalism and dismissed Democratic opponents as "English free traders." Republicans thought free trade led inexorably to low wages and economic ruin. Protectionism was associated with prosperity and independence.[45]

Thus, he says, preaching class harmony, nineteenth-century Republican economic nationalists justified the protective tariff as essential for protecting domestic workers from imports made by cheap European labor—essentially the same argument Buchanan makes today. They considered the tariff a fee on foreign manufacturers for participating in the American market.

Lincoln, the first Republican president, advocated a moderate tariff. He adhered to the view that the "abandonment of the protective policy must result in the increase of idleness and so in proportion must produce want and ruin among our people."[46]

William McKinley, who as an Ohio congressman sponsored the McKinley Tariff, enjoyed castigating Democratic free traders. In one famous speech, he warned in remarkably Buchanan-like language: "Free trade will bring widespread discontent. It will revolutionize values. It will take away more than one half of the earning capacity of brain and brawn."[47]

Theodore Roosevelt, a particular hero of Buchanan's, expressed similar sympathies. In 1895, he wrote a friend: "Thank God I am not a free trader. In this country, pernicious indulgence in the doctrine of free trade seems inevitably to produce fatty degeneration of the moral fiber."[48]

According to Eckes, from 1860 to 1932, the high-tariff card worked well for Republican candidates. Republicans won fourteen of eighteen presidential elections. Democrats, portrayed as dupes of English free-trade theorists, achieved few victories until the 1912 struggle between Theodore Roosevelt and William Howard Taft split the Republican vote, paving the way for Woodrow Wilson, who then reduced the tariffs on dutiable goods from an average of 41 percent to 27 percent.

The resulting concern about cheap imports, as well as opposition to the League of Nations, gave Republicans a rallying cry during the unpopular Wilson years. Thus, the 1920 Republican convention and its candidate, Warren C. Harding, reaffirmed the party's long-held commitment to the protective tariff. His landslide victory led to the passage of the Fordney-McCumber Act in 1922, which raised tariff rates on dutiable goods without depressing the quantity of imports or disrupting world trade.

Republicans remained solid protectionists until after the Second World War. Then, Dwight Eisenhower, purportedly concerned about helping our Allies and former adversaries recover from the war, switched sides of the aisle on the issue. Thus, he initiated the first tariff-cutting program.

Interestingly, according to Eckes, one of the last articulate Republican trade nationalists was Prescott Bush, a senator from Connecticut and George Bush's father.

The question is, Do elements of traditional economic nationalism offer a road map for the current spate of trade woes in this country? Eckes maintains, "The record appears to show that it has served the Republican Party and the country well." In fact, he says: "In the generation after 1870, America protected its market and experienced economic growth more than double that of free-trade England."[49]

Thus, according to California congressman Duncan Hunter, "Pat Buchanan is the one guy in the Republican field who understands trade and how important it is."[50]

Campaign lore has it that Buchanan found his economic populist heart campaigning in New Hampshire shortly after announcing his first bid for the Republican nomination on December 10, 1991. Visiting a paper mill in Groveton, New Hampshire, where 350 people had been laid off earlier in the day, Buchanan approached a line of workers awaiting their Christmas turkeys. One man looked at him and said, "Save our jobs." Recalling the incident when he declared his candidacy anew in 1995 Buchanan said it had convinced him that government "is frozen in the ice of indifference" when it comes to workers' problems.[51]

Although Buchanan was clearly moved by the recession's human toll in New Hampshire, he has actually always had a populist streak. As early as 1970 he wrote Richard Nixon an eleven-page memo advising him to exploit politically the populist resentments of the working class: "We should aim our strategy primarily at disaffected Democrats, at blue-collar workers, and at working-class ethnics. We should set out to capture the vote of the 47-year-old Dayton housewife."[52]

This was the heart and soul of the "Silent Majority" strategy that Buchanan crafted for Nixon's convincing victories over Hubert Humphrey and George McGovern.

Buchanan would later offer similar advice to Ronald Reagan, stressing the political emotions of the disaffected. And Reagan took his counsel on a number of key policy items.

Buchanan wears this heritage proudly:

Yes, Ronald Reagan preached free trade, but he also imposed quotas on imported autos, steel and machine tools, and slammed a 50 percent tariff on motor bikes to keep Tokyo's predators from killing Harley-Davidson. Every industry Reagan "protected" was restored to health. Should we have abandoned them to massage the ideology of kennel-fed conservatives who celebrate "market forces" from their endowed and upholstered chairs at think tanks?[53]

His is a point well taken in this day of stiff global competition: "Every nation to rise to industrial power in modern times—Britain before 1850, America and Germany between 1865 and 1914, postwar Japan—did so by first protecting the home market."[54]

For all their talk of heresy, it appears that the neoconservative establishment now in control of the Republican Party is actually significantly more out of step with the GOP's conservative traditions than is Buchanan.

Moral Issues

To hear some tell it, Pat Buchanan's frightful unfitness for elective office is best exemplified by his extremist positions on moral and cultural issues. On the plaguing questions of abortion, family values, homosexuality, criminal conduct, and education he has, they say, crossed the Styx into a nether realm of intolerance.

But, as columnist Cal Thomas asks, Just who are the real extremists in America?

PAT ANSWERS

91

Is it the ones who want to reestablish concepts such as right and wrong in our schools, or those who kicked out the Bible and put in condoms and weapon detectors? The ones whose curriculum produced well-educated young people, or those whose ideas have given us functional illiterates who can barely read their worthless high school diplomas? Which extreme is to be blamed for family breakup? Those who opposed no-fault divorce, or those who supported it, along with prenuptial agreements and cohabitation? Which extreme is responsible for the growing underclass? The poverty merchants whose idea of compassion is to raise taxes, redistribute your income, or those who see much—but not all—poverty resulting from bad lifestyle choices encouraged by popular culture? Which extreme created cities whose streets are unsafe to navigate at night? Which extreme is responsible for a judicial system that has been transformed into a servant of opinion polls and social engineers?[55]

Indeed, he asks, "Which is a more extreme family role model: Ozzie and Harriet or Beavis and Butt-head?"[56]

Those are the kinds of questions Buchanan has been asking for years as the point man for traditional values in the wide-ranging culture war in America. His famed Houston speech was but one shot in a consistent salvo of assaults on the vested interests of ethical latitudinarianism and moral mendacity.

Responding to Mario Cuomo's charge that such concerns smack of fascism,[57] Buchanan replied with a scathing yet eloquent editorial.

Mario is not the only one to have recoiled in fear and loathing. Media who have burbled all over Mario's locutions in class warfare found my Houston speech "divisive," "hateful," and the old standby, "racist." Carl Rowan told his co-panelists on *Inside Washington* it was the closest he had ever heard to a Nazi address. Bob Beckel thought my remarks might have been ghosted by Satan himself.

The savagery of the reaction—ongoing—underscores my point: as polarized as we have ever been, we Americans are locked in a cultural war for the soul of our country.

What is it all about? As columnist Sam Francis writes, it is about power; it is about who determines "the norms by which we live, and by which we define and govern ourselves." Who decides what is right and wrong, moral and immoral, beautiful and ugly, healthy and sick? Whose beliefs shall form the basis of law?

At Houston, William Rusher writes, America heard "the first rumbles of a new storm fast approaching the American political arena—a storm that will quickly replace the old battles over the conduct of the cold war." Indeed, the storm has already hit the coast.

The Bosnia of the cultural war is abortion.

The Republican Party, in platform and ticket, is pro-life. In other words, we hold abortion to be the unjust killing of a pre-born child. Bill Clinton's party rejoices in Roe v. Wade. To the one side, the 25 million abortions in 20 years are a testament to freedom and progress; to the other, they are the benchmark of a society literally hell-bent on suicide. The conflicting positions can no more be reconciled than those of John Brown and John Calhoun.

Whose side is God on? In an angry letter to President Bush, the National Council of Churches wrote: "We need to be very clear that God belongs to no one side, for we believe all belong to God." Mr. Bush's effort to conscript Him, they wrote, is blasphemous.

But was it blasphemous to enlist Him at Selma Bridge? Is the Creator truly neutral in the unequal struggle between his tiniest creatures and the abortionist with knife and suction pump?

To those gathered at Madison Square Garden, a man's "sexual preference" and sexual conduct, so long as it is consensual, is irrelevant to moral character. To most of us in Houston, however, it is the codification of amorality to elevate gay liaisons to the same moral and legal plane as traditional marriage.

Americans are a tolerant people. But a majority believes that the sexual practices of gays, whether a result of nature or nurture, are both morally wrong and medically ruinous. Many consider this "reactionary" or "homophobic." But our beliefs are rooted in the Old and New Testament, in natural law and tradition, even in the writing of that paragon of the Enlightenment, Thomas Jefferson—who felt homosexuality should be punished as severely as rape.

Thirty years ago, both sides in today's cultural war shared the belief that homosexuals, be they 2 or 10 percent of the population, had the same constitutional rights as the rest of us, as well as a right to be let alone. We still do. Homosexuality was not an issue then. What makes it an issue now is the non-negotiable demand that this "lifestyle" be sanctioned by law, that gays be granted equal rights to marry, adopt and serve as troop leaders in the Boy Scouts.

Let me be blunt: we can't support this. To force it upon us is like forcing Christians to burn incense to the emperor.

But the cultural war is broader than two battle-grounds.

We see it in the altered calendar of holidays we are invited—nay, instructed—to celebrate. Washington's Birthday disappears into Presidents' Day. States, like Arizona, that balk at declaring Martin Luther King's birthday a holiday face political censure and convention boycotts. Easter is displaced by Earth Day, Christmas becomes Winter Break, Columbus Day a day to reflect on the cultural imperialism and genocidal racism of the "dead white males" who raped this continent while exterminating its noblest inhabitants.

Secularism's Holy Days of Obligation were not demanded by us; they were imposed on us. And while Governor Cuomo may plausibly plead ignorance of the culture war, the Hard Left has always understood its criticality.

"Give me the child for six years," Lenin reportedly said, quoting the Jesuits, "and he will be a Marxist forever." J. V. Stalin, who was partial to Chicago gangster films, thought that if only he had control of Hollywood, he could control the world.

"Too many conservatives," writes art critic James Cooper, "never read Mao Tse-Tung on waging cultural war against the West. Mao's essays were prescribed reading for the Herbert Marcuse-generation of the 1960s, who now run our cultural institutions. Conservatives were oblivious to the fact that modern art—long ago separated from the idealism of Monet, Degas, Cezanne, and Rodin—had become the purveyor of a destructive, degenerate, ugly, pornographic, Marxist, anti-American ideology." While we were off aiding the Contras, a Fifth Column inside our own country was capturing the culture.

In wartime and postwar movies, the USA was a land worth fighting for, even dying for. But the distance from *The Sands of Iwo Jima* to *Born on the Fourth of July*, from *The Song of Bernadette* to *The Last Temptation of Christ*, which paints Jesus as a lustful, lying wimp, is more than four decades. Hollywood has crossed a cultural and religious divide—and left us on the other side.

In Eddie Murphy's new film, *Boomerang*, every successful black has one obsession: having good sex, and lots of it. I left thinking this film could have been produced by the KKK, so thoroughly did it conform to old Klan propaganda about blacks being little more than sexual animals. From *The Cosby Show* to *Boomerang* is straight downhill; it is to travel from what is decent to what is decadent.

A sense of shame presupposes a set of standards. In the Old America, Ingrid Bergman, carrying the child of her lover, fled the country in scandal. Today, she would probably be asked to pose naked—and nine months' pregnant—on the cover of *Vanity Fair*.

Today, the standards are gone. Does it make a difference? Only if you believe books and plays and films and art make a difference in men's lives. Only if you believe ideas have consequences.

In *The End of Christendom,* the late Malcolm Mugge-ridge wrote that Dostoevsky, in his astoundingly pro-phetic novel *The Devils* makes his character Peter Vekovinsky say, "A generation or two of debauchery fol-lowed by a little sweet bloodletting and the turmoil will begin." So indeed it has.

"Poets are the unacknowledged legislators of the world," wrote poet Shelley. Does it make a difference that school kids in LA, who never heard of Robert Frost, can recite the lyrics of Ice-T and 2 Live Crew? Ask the people of Koreatown.

Where did that LA mob come from? It came out of the public schools from which the Bible and Ten Com-mandments were long ago expelled. It came out of drug-stores where pornography is everywhere on the magazine rack. It came out of movie theaters and away from TV sets where sex and violence are romanticized. It came out of rock concerts where rap music extols raw lust and cop-killing. It came out of churches that long ago gave them-selves up to social action, and it came out of families that never existed.

When the Rodney King verdict came down, and the rage boiled with, these young men had no answer within themselves to the question: Why not? Why not loot and burn? Why not settle accounts with the Koreans? Why not lynch somebody—and get even for Rodney King?

The secularists who have captured our culture have substituted a New Age Gospel, with its governing axi-oms: There are no absolute values in the universe; there are no fixed and objective standards of right and wrong. There is no God. It all begins here and it ends here. Every man lives by his own moral code. Do your own thing. Well, the mob took them at their word and did its own thing.

"Of all the dispositions and habits which lead to prosperity," Washington said, "religion and morality are indispensable supports. In vain would that man seek the tribute of patriotism, who should labor to subvert these great pillars of human happiness."

Look at the works of "art" that ignited the controversy at the National Endowment. Almost all were desecrations of Christian images. Andreas Serrano submerged a crucifix in a vat of his own urine. Robert Mapplethorpe took a statue of the Virgin Mother of God and twisted it into a bloody tie rack.

Writing in an art catalog funded by NEA, an AIDS activist called Cardinal John O'Connor a "fat cannibal from that house of walking swastikas up on Fifth Avenue." That "house of walking swastikas" was St. Patrick's Cathedral, subsequently desecrated by militants who spat consecrated hosts on the floor at Sunday Mass.

Yes, Mario, there is a connection.

The cultural war is already raging in our public schools. In history texts Benedict Arnold's treason at West Point has been dropped. So has the story of Nathan Hale, the boy-patriot who spied on the British and went to the gallows with the defiant cry, "I regret that I have but one life to give for my country." Elsewhere, they teach that our constitution was plagiarized from the Iroquois, that Western science was stolen from sub-Sahara Africa.

The name Custer has been stricken from the battlefield where his unit fell. Demands are heard throughout the South that replicas of the Battle Flag of the Confederacy be removed from state flags and public buildings. The old iron Confederate soldier who stood for decades in the town square must be removed; after all, he fought in an ignoble cause.

Slavery vs. freedom, that's all it was about, they tell us. But go up to Gettysburg and park your car behind the union center. Look across that mile-long field and visualize 15,000 men and boys forming up at the tree line. See them walking across into the fire of cannon and gun, knowing they would never get back, never see home again. Nine of ten never even owned a slave. They were fighting for the things for which men have always fought: family, faith, friends, and country. For the ashes of their fathers and the temples of their Gods.

If a country forgets where it came from, how will its people know who they are? Will America one day become like that poor old man with Alzheimer's abandoned in the stadium, who did not know where he came from, or to what family he belonged? The battle over our schools is part of the war to separate parents from children, one generation from another, and all Americans from their heritage.

Our "common difficulties concern, thank God, only material things," FDR said at the nadir of the Depression. Our national quarrel goes much deeper. It is about who we are and what we believe. Are we any longer "one nation under God," or has one-half of that nation already begun to secede from the other?

That, Mario, is what the cultural war is all about.[58]

Educated by Jesuits, Buchanan was exposed early on to the writing and teaching of Augustine of Hippo. He

was one of the greatest men and most brilliant minds
Africa ever produced—standing shoulder to shoulder
with such greats as Athanasius, Origen, and Tertullian.
He was born in 354 at Tagaste—in present-day Alge-
ria—of a pagan father and a Christian mother. He was
brought up as a Christian but not baptized.

He studied rhetoric at the great University of Car-
thage in order to become a lawyer, but later gave up his
plan to for a career in teaching. His study of philosophy—with an emphasis on Platonism and Manichaean-
ism—resulted in a complete renunciation of Christianity.
He lived a self-confessed debauched life—including
keeping a mistress for fifteen years by whom he had a
son.

In pursuit of opportunities to improve his academic
standing, Augustine took teaching posts—first in Rome
and later in Milan. It was in this latter city that he fell
under the sway of the great bishop and rhetorician Ambrose. After a long battle of the soul—described in his
classic work *Confessions*—Augustine was converted under Ambrose's ministry and was baptized in 386.

After two years of intensive discipling and catechizing,
he returned to Africa and established a quasi-monastic
community in Hippo. There he founded his famous
Classicum Academae—devoted to study, writing, and
the work of cultural transformation. The school was
famed for its emphasis on art, music, politics, and ideas.

In 391 the steadfastness, holiness, and giftedness of
Augustine was recognized and he was ordained against
his own objections. In 394 he was elevated as coadjutor

in the diocese. And in 396 he was elevated to the bish-opric of the city.

Most of his brilliant writings have endured the test of time—I have eight thick volumes that sit on my desk—and are widely read to this day. His commentaries—on Genesis and Psalms particularly—are of inestimable value. His apologetics—like his *Contra Manichae* or *Contra Pelagae*—continue to set the standard for ortho-doxy. And his didactae—like his *Sanctus Dei* or *De Trin-itate*—formed the first, and arguably the best, systematic theologies the church has ever produced.

But Augustine is perhaps best known for—and made his greatest contribution with—his analysis of the cul-ture war here on earth and its relation to the war in the heavenlies. Entitled *De Civitate Dei*—or *The City of God*—the book continues to define the terms of the de-bate better than any other work written before or since.

According to Augustine, cultures are not reflections of a people's race, ethnicity, folklore, politics, language, or heritage. Rather they are outworkings of a people's creed. In other words, culture is the temporal manifesta-tion of a people's faith. If a culture begins to change, it is not because of fads, fashions, or the passing of time, it is because of a shift in worldview—it is because of a change of faith. Thus, race, ethnicity, folklore, politics, lan-guage, or heritage are simply expressions of a deeper paradigm rooted in the covenantal and spiritual matrix of a community's church and the integrity of its witness.

The reason that Augustine spent so much of his life and ministry critiquing the pagan philosophies of the world and exposing the aberrant theologies of the church was that he understood only too well that those things matter not only in the realm of eternity, determining the spiritual destiny of masses of humanity, but in the realm of the here and now, determining the temporal destiny of whole civilizations.

Unlike Tertullian, who decried the cultural applicability of the church asking, "What hath Athens to do with Jerusalem?" Augustine recognized that a people's dominant worldview inevitably shapes the world they have in view. And he also recognized that the church is the genesis point for the development of that worldview as it faithfully fulfills its calling to do justice, love mercy, and walk humbly with Almighty God.

Bridging the gap between activism and devotion, the Christian social teaching that Buchanan was nurtured in—very much rooted in Augustine's teaching—describes a comprehensive and integrated worldview of vital faith and meaningful cultural activity. It presents what C. S. Lewis called "Mere Christianity,"[59] what John Stott called "Basic Christianity,"[60] and what William Wilberforce called "Real Christianity."[61] It delineates the ingredients of a balanced life—of integrated spiritual, moral, and cultural concerns.

Writing to one of her many literary friends, the remarkable blind, deaf, and mute Helen Keller reflected upon this notion:

> I long to accomplish a great and noble task, but it is my chief duty to accomplish humble tasks as though they

were great and noble. The world is moved along not by the mighty shoves of its heroes, but by the aggregate of the tiny pushes of each honest worker.[62]

If that be extremism, then so be it.

Issue by Issue

Pat Buchanan's many and varied concerns have meant that he has commented on virtually every issue imaginable. His prolificacy means that even the broadest selection of his pronouncements can only be a sampling.[63]

America First: "We need a new foreign policy that ends foreign aid and pulls up all the trip wires laid down abroad to involve American soldiers in wars that are none of America's business. And we need to demand that rich allies begin paying the full cost of their own defense."[64]

Social Security: "This is another area where I part company with many of my colleagues. They want to offset the Republican tax cuts by cutting cost-of-living adjustments for Social Security. I say Congress has an obligation to totally zero-out foreign aid, and cancel the $20 billion Mexican bailout, before it takes one penny out of the pockets of retired Americans who have paid Social Security taxes their entire lives."[65]

Global Trade Agreements: "When I am elected president of the United States, there will be no more NAFTA sellouts of American workers. There will be no more GATT deals done for the benefit of Wall Street bankers.

And there will be no more $50 billion bailouts of Third World socialists, whether in Moscow or Mexico City."[66]

Foreign Lobbyists: "In a Buchanan White House, foreign lobbyists and corporate contributors will not sit at the head of the table. I will. We're going to bring the jobs home and we're going to keep America's jobs here, and when I walk into the Oval Office, we start looking out for America first."[67]

Defense: "Rogue nations that despise America, right now, are plotting to build weapons of mass destruction and to buy or to build the missiles to deliver them to our country. Yet the United States of America remains naked to a missile attack. We have no defense. Why? Because a twenty-year-old compact with a cheating Soviet regime that has been dead half a decade prevents us from building our missile defense. Well, that dereliction of duty ends the day I take the oath. I will maintain a military for the United States that is first on the land, first on the seas, first in the air, first in space—and I will not ask any nation's permission before I build a missile defense for the United States of America."[68]

Free Trade: "Rather than making global free trade a golden calf which we all bow down to and worship, all trade deals should be judged by whether: A) they maintain U.S. sovereignty, B) they protect vital economic interests, and C) they ensure a rising standard of living for all our workers. We must stop sacrificing American jobs on the altars of trans-national corporations whose sole loyalty is to the bottom line."[69]

Mexican Bailout: "This deal represents our first payment on NAFTA and GATT. The looting of America, on behalf of the New World Order, has begun. That Mr. Clinton would take such risks for the former clients of Robert Rubin shows both the desperation and the determination to make good their losses of the Wall Street contributors who have their hooks deep in the flesh of both national parties. This deal isn't a loan. It isn't an investment in the future. It is a $48 billion wash rag to wipe the egg off the faces of the politicians who marched us into NAFTA and GATT. President Clinton may have circumvented Congress in this bailout, but the Republican-controlled 104th Congress is not impotent. It should act now to make good its mandate to make government accountable."[70]

Jobs: "What is an economy for if not so that workers and their families can enjoy the good life their parents knew, so that incomes rise with every year of hard work, and so that Americans once again enjoy the highest standard of living in the world? Our American workers are the most productive in the world; our technology is the finest. Yet, the real incomes of American workers have fallen 20 percent in twenty years. Why are our people not realizing the fruits of their labor? We have a government that is frozen in the ice of its own indifference, a government that does not listen anymore to the forgotten men and women who work in the forges and factories and plants and businesses of this country. We have, instead, a government that is too busy taking the phone calls from lobbyists for foreign countries and the corporate contributors of the Fortune 500."[71]

Taxes: "Bob Dole and Phil Gramm are friends of mine. They are good men. But they are both Big Government Republicans. When the crunch came in 1990, and every conservative worth his salt was fighting against George Bush's tax increase, Bob and Phil were on the other side. They urged George Bush to break his no-new-taxes pledge—the decision that destroyed the Reagan coalition. They also both supported the huge tax increases of the early 1980s. If the record shows that you have repeatedly supported huge tax increases as a member of Congress, why should we believe that you are going to resist them as president? American society is over-regulated, overtaxed, overburdened by government. We need tax cuts across the board, and an end to the bias in the tax code against investment and saving. The IRS needs to be downsized. And any Balanced Budget Amendment must have a tax limitation provision so politicians cannot use it to raise the government's share of the people's income."[72]

Judicial Reform: "Supreme Court justices and federal judges have grabbed more power, far more, than the Constitution intended. We should strip that power away through judicial term limits, voter recall of renegade federal jurists, and reconfirmation of Supreme Court Justices every eight years. We must never forget that it wasn't voters who legalized abortion across America—it was the black-robed politicians on the Supreme Court. Let's put these arrogant justices, and their junior partners on the inferior courts, back into the tiny corner of power set aside for them by the Constitution. Supreme

Court justices should be reconfirmed every eight years; and there should be an eight-year-term limit on federal judges. And the American people as a whole should be able to do what Californians already have the power to do when their judges become tyrants: Recall and fire them."[73]

Equal Justice under the Law: "Reverse discrimination by quota, contract set-aside, busing, affirmative action are un-American. We need to outlaw the federal classification of American citizens by race or ethnicity and end all discrimination and all preferential treatment."[74]

Affirmative Action: "With the court's recent decisions, an opportunity is at hand to advance the constitutional idea of a color-blind nation by uprooting all forms of ethnic and racial discrimination from our national government and abolishing set-asides, quotas, diversity programs, and all of the other odious paraphernalia of reverse discrimination. Affirmative action, no matter how benign its original purpose, belongs in the same graveyard as its cousin, the late Jim Crow. It is time to put an end to hyphenated Americanism. It is time that, together, we Americans advanced toward the great and good ideal that, no matter where our kinfolk came from, we are all one American family and one people with the same constitutional and civil rights."[75]

Tax-Funded Arts: "All federally funded institutions, from the Smithsonian to the National Endowment for the Arts, will manifest a respect for America's history and values; and all monuments, battlefields, and symbols of

America's glorious, if sometimes tragic, history will be protected."[76]

Education: "Parents everywhere are fighting for the hearts and minds of their own children. We must shut down the Department of Education and return authority to the states and to the people."[77]

Abortion: "We must reverse *Roe v. Wade,* persevere in the fight for life, and restore to our parents and communities the freedom to clean up the cultural pollution poisoning the hearts and minds of our children. The presidency must become a bully pulpit for traditional values, not gays in the military. We will keep the Republican Party solidly in the pro-life camp, and get the U.S. government completely out of the abortion racket."[78]

Defunding Planned Parenthood: "Not one dime of taxpayer money will go to Planned Parenthood. Not one dime to UNFPA. Not one dime to fetal-tissue research. And not one dime to research that uses human embryos."[79]

Human Life Hearings: "In the twenty-two years since *Roe v. Wade,* the technology has developed to dramatically demonstrate the humanity of the child originating in the womb. Our Republican Congress must hold hearings, using this technology, and calling on biologists, doctors, and ethicists, to teach America the truth that every abortion stops a beating heart."[80]

Victimization of Women: "We must hold hearings on women victimized by abortion. Congress must listen to their stories. We need to hear from the women who have suffered depression, had suicidal tendencies, taken to alcohol—after an abortion. And we need to investigate the health consequences for these women—the illnesses, the infections, the likelihood of breast cancer."[81]

Heritage: "When many of us were young, public schools and Catholic schools, Christian schools and Jewish schools, instructed children in their religious heritage and Judeo-Christian values, in what was right and what was wrong. We were taught about the greatness and goodness of this land we call God's country, in which we are all so fortunate to live. But today, in too many of our schools, our children are being robbed of their innocence. Their minds are being poisoned against their Judeo-Christian heritage, against America's heroes and against American history, against the values of faith and family and country. Eternal truths that do not change from the Old and New Testament have been expelled from our public schools, and our children are being indoctrinated in moral relativism, and the propaganda of an anti-Western ideology."[82]

Immigration Control: "Illegal immigration must be halted and no illegal alien given welfare. We need a nationwide Proposition 187, a closing of the Southwest border to illegals—with the National Guard if necessary—and a new immigration law where we Americans decide who comes, and when. Our first concern must be the peace, stability, and unity of our own country. Every year millions of undocumented aliens break our laws, cross our borders, and demand social benefits paid for with the tax dollars of American citizens. California is being bankrupted. Texas, Florida, and Arizona are begging Washington to do its duty and defend the states as the Constitution requires. Yet our leaders, timid and fearful of being called names, do nothing. Well, they have not invented the name I have not been called. So the Custodians of Political Correctness do not frighten me. And I will do what is necessary to defend the borders of my country even if it means putting the National Guard all along our southern frontier."[83]

Reinventing Constitutionalism: " 'In questions of power,' said Jefferson, 'let us hear no more of trust in men, but rather, bind them down from mischief with the chains of the Constitution.' We need term limits on all members of Congress and all our federal judges."[84]

Second Amendment: "As President, Bill Clinton has repeatedly attacked the right of law-abiding Americans to keep and bear arms through both the Brady Act and the ban on certain semiautomatic guns. The semiautomatic ban is an unambiguous violation of the Second Amendment. The Brady Act violates not only the Second Amendment but the Tenth by imposing an unfunded mandate on local law enforcement agencies. The Republican Congress should repeal both laws and challenge Mr. Clinton's veto threats. As president, I would use all the constitutional powers of that office to ensure that the rights of American gun owners, as provided for in the Bill of Rights, are fully and faithfully protected."[85]

Sovereignty: "We Americans must also start recapturing our lost national sovereignty. The men who stood at Lexington and at Concord Bridge, at Bunker Hill and Saratoga, they gave all they had, that the land they loved might be a free, independent, sovereign nation. Yet today, our birthright of sovereignty, purchased with the blood of patriots, is being traded away for foreign money, handed over to faceless foreign bureaucrats at places like the IMF, the World Bank, the World Trade Organization and the U.N."[86]

United Nations: "A year ago, two United States helicopters flying surveillance over northern Iraq were shot down by American fighter planes in a terrible incident of friendly fire. Captain Patrick McKenna of the Citadel, where I just visited, commanded one of those helicopters. Every American on board was killed. And when the story hit the news, the vice president, then visiting in Marrakesh at the World Trade Organization meeting, issued a statement that said the parents of these young men and women can be proud their sons and daughters died in the service of the United Nations. But those young men and women didn't take an oath to the United Nations. They took an oath to defend the Constitution and the country we love. And let me say to you, when Pat Buchanan gets into that Oval Office as Commander-in-Chief, no young men and women will ever be sent into battle except under American officers and to fight under the American flag."[87]

Tenth Amendment: "Many functions of the federal government are, *de facto,* unconstitutional, wholesale violations of the Tenth Amendment that reserves such powers to the states. The federal government should be cut, with Cabinet departments abolished, the money

they spend returned to citizens, the duties they assumed
returned to the states."[88]

According to Joe Sobran:

> One of the nicer charges against Pat Buchanan is that he
> is a "bully." This is just about the opposite of the truth.
> A bully picks fights he knows he can win; Buchanan picks
> fights with forces larger than himself. The truth is that
> Buchanan has the type of personality, common among
> the Irish, that looks threatening to the sort of people
> who don't like to fight at all, unless they enjoy the safety
> of belonging to a mob—which pretty well describes most
> journalists. He loves to fight. He is ashamed to fight
> anyone weaker than himself; he regards it as a matter of
> honor, and fun, to mix it up with something bigger than
> he is. There is no glory in bullying, but there is glory in
> losing in a good cause. It's the glory of martyrdom. If
> you saw the movie *Braveheart,* you saw Buchanan's
> ideal.[89]

Indeed, based on the issues he has attached his name
to alone, Pat Buchanan has proven himself to be of that
William Wallace/*Braveheart* ilk.

CHAPTER 5

The New Conservatism of the Heart

There are those who believe that a new modernity demands a new morality. What they fail to consider is the harsh reality that there is no such thing as a new morality. There is only one morality. All else is immorality. There is only true Christian ethics over against which stands the whole of paganism. If we are to fulfill our great destiny as a people, then we must return to the old morality, the sole morality.

—Theodore Roosevelt[1]

In a remarkably insightful essay in the neo-conservative journal *Weekly Standard*, David Brooks identifies one of the most interesting ironies of Patrick Buchanan's populist campaign:

He says his followers are peasants. He speaks for working men and their grievances. He rails and rouses audiences like a carnival barker. But Pat Buchanan's presidential run is in fact as close to an intellectual's campaign as we have seen in modern politics.[2]

Indeed, the campaign that Buchanan has put together hardly resembles a political campaign at all. It is practically devoid of all the trappings of the partisan hustings—including the fund-raising machine. Instead, it more closely resembles a traveling think tank:

> The Buchanan campaign doesn't have a pollster, nor does it have much in the way of consultants and apparatchiks. Instead, it has writers. His campaign manager Terry Jeffrey spent four years writing editorials for the *Washington Times.* His staffer Justin Raimondo wrote a definitive history of the Old Right. His friends and propagandists, such as Thomas Flemming and Samuel Francis, are essayists, as is Buchanan himself.[3]

As a result, the campaign is both colorful and creative. It is also substantive and deep: "Huey Long and other populists may have tossed off their rhetoric from the top of their head. But Buchanan's rhetoric and ideas have an intellectual pedigree."[4]

Thus, when Buchanan declaims about the coursings of the Culture War, or about the role of women in society, or about keeping America first, or about the primacy of faith, family, and work, he is working in part from ideas studiously developed over a long period of time. He is working from an established intellectual tradition.

And what is that tradition? According to Samuel Francis:

> The core of his message consists of a rejection of the thinly masked economic determinism espoused by

Kemp, Gramm, and Gingrich and an affirmation of the primacy of cultural identity, national sovereignty, and national interests over economic goals. The Culture War for Buchanan is not Republican swaggering about family values and dirty movies but a battle over whether the nation itself can continue to exist under the onslaught of the militant secularism, acquisitive egoism, economic and political globalism, demographic inundation, and unchecked state centralism supported by the Ruling Class.[5]

This presuppositional system is what Russell Kirk called "reflective conservatism," what Murray Rothbard called "paelo-conservatism," and what Ronald Reagan called the "old right." It is what Buchanan calls the "new conservatism of the heart." It is a system that consists of at least six premises or axioms, according to Kirk:

First, such conservatives generally believe that there exists a transcendent moral order, to which we ought to try to conform the ways of society. A divine tactic, however dimly descried, is at work in human society.[6]

Second, such conservatives uphold the principle of social continuity. They prefer the devil they know to the devil they don't know. Order, and justice, and freedom, they believe, are the artificial products of a long and painful social experience, the results of centuries of trial and reflection and sacrifice.[7]

Third, such conservatives believe in what may be called the principle of prescription. "The wisdom of our ancestors" is one of the more important phrases in the writings of Burke; presumably Burke derived it from Richard

Hooker. Conservatives sense that modern men are dwarfs on the shoulders of giants, able to see farther than their ancestors only because of the great stature of those who have preceded us in time. Therefore conservatives very frequently emphasize the importance of prescription—that is, of things established by immemorial usage, so that "the mind runneth not to the contrary." There exist rights of which the chief sanction is their antiquity.[8]

Fourth, such conservatives are guided by their principle of prudence. Any public measure ought to be judged by its probable long-run consequences, not merely by temporary advantage or popularity. Human society being complex, remedies cannot be simple if they are to be effective.[9]

Fifth, such conservatives pay attention to the principle of variety. They feel affection for the proliferating intricacy of long-established social institutions and modes of life, as distinguished from the narrowing uniformity and deadening egalitarianism of radical systems.[10]

Sixth, such conservatives are chastened by their principle of imperfectibility. Human nature suffers irremediably from certain faults, the conservatives know. Man being imperfect, no perfect social order ever can be created. To aim at utopia is to end in disaster.[11]

This estimation of life, rooted in the philosophical consensus of Christendom, is thus naturally the very opposite—indeed the negation—of the stock and trade of virtually all twentieth-century political systems ideology. As a result, this peculiar form of conservatism tends to take the guise of contrarianism.

Against the Tide

In the twentieth century, the smothering influence of ideological politics is everywhere evident. It has all too evidently wrested control of every academic discipline, of every cultural trend, of every intellectual impulse, even of every religious revival in our time. From Nazism and Stalinism to pluralism and multiculturalism, from liberalism and conservatism to monopolism and socialism, ours has been an epoch of movements beguiled by the temporal seductions of ideological politics.

Nearly every question, every issue, every social dilemma has been and continues to be translated into legal, juridical, or mechanical terms. They are supplied with bureaucratic, mathematical, or systemic solutions. If there is something wrong with the economy, then government must fix it. If family values are absent, then government must supply them. If health-care provision is inefficient, then government must rectify the situation. If education is in disarray, then government must reorder the system. Whatever the problem, it seems that government is the solution.

Virtually all social historians agree that this is indeed the most distinctive aspect of our age: the subsuming of all other concerns to the rise of political mass movements based upon comprehensive, secular, closed-universe, and millenarian intellectual systems. Thus, at one time or another, Henry David Aiken, Karl Dietrich Bracher, Isaac Kraminick, Frederick Watkins, Barbara Tuchman, Antonia Fraser, Paul Johnson, Russell Kirk, and Murray Rothbard have all dubbed this the "Age of Ideology."[12]

The name of the ideological game is power. With all the cool detachment of wintry witchery every other consideration is relegated to a piratical humbug. G. K. Chesterton observes:

> There is, as a ruling element in modern life, a blind and asinine appetite for mere power. There is a spirit abroad among the nations of the earth which drives men incessantly on to destroy what they cannot understand, and to capture what they cannot enjoy.[13]

According to philosopher Eric Voegelin, this awful tendency "is essentially the politics of spiritual revolt."[14] It is, he says, a kind of a "psychic disorientation,"[15] a "metastatic faith,"[16] a "modern promethianism,"[17] a "secular parousianism,"[18] or, perhaps most accurately, a "dominion of pneumapathological consciousness."[19]

Elaborating on those notions, political scientist Michael Franz has said:

> Ideological consciousness is typified by a turning-away from the transcendent ground in revolt against the tension of contingent existence. In the modern era this revolt has taken many forms, all of which are expressive of dissatisfaction with the degree of certainty afforded by faith, trust, and hope as sources of knowledge and existential orientation. The great ideologists seek to displace Christian revelation by misplacing the transcendent ground within an immanent hierarchy of being, identify-

ing the essence of human existence as productive relations, historical progress, racial compensation, libidinous
drives, scientific rationality, or the will to power. Within
the intellectual systems constructed around these mis-
placements of the ground, humanity appears as an auton-
omous, self-created species capable of assuming control
of its destiny through the self-conscious application of
new forms of knowledge.[20]

In short, ideological politics is little more than a re-
vived gnosticism, an abiding humanism rooted in the
naked politicalization of every detail of life. It is a
worldview as thorough and as dominating in our time as
was the Faith during the epoch of Christendom.

Thus Jane Addams—the radical urban social reformer
during the uproarious teens and twenties—was hardly
exaggerating when she said: "Ideology is the modern
ecology. It is the landscape we see, the sound we hear,
the food we eat, the air we breathe. It is the incarnation
of truth for us and the emblem and impress of earthly
harmony. It is the essence of modern beauty."[21]

To make matters worse, twentieth-century ideology
was wed to a worldview of relentless social Darwinism
bent on enforcing a kind of cultural "survival of the
nastiest."

It was a system of thought rooted in the superiority—
even the supremacy—of science over every other discipline or concern. A fantastic world could be expected in
the days just ahead because the sovereign prerogative of
science would, no doubt, make short work of curing

every cultural ill, correcting every irrational thought, and subverting every cantankerous disturbance. There was no obstacle too great, no objection too considerable, and no resistance too substantial to restrain the onward and upward march of the scientific evolution of human society.

That kind of unswerving confidence in the good providence of industry and technology gave its adherents a conceited algebraic certainty about their forecasts and predictions. As H. G. Wells, one of the leading lights of such sanguine futurism, asserted:

> For some of us moderns, who have been touched with the spirit of science, prophesying is almost a habit of mind. Science is very largely analysis aimed at forecasting. The test of any scientific law is our verification of its anticipations. The scientific training develops the idea that whatever is going to happen is really here now—if only one could see it. And when one is taken by surprise, the tendency is not to say with the untrained man, "Now, who'd ha' thought it?" but "Now, what was it we overlooked?" Everything that has ever existed or that will ever exist is here—for anyone who has eyes to see. But some of it demands eyes of superhuman penetration.[22]

For Wells, and all those who shared his Flash Gordon optimism, science was a kind of new secular predestination. It not only affirmed what could be, it confirmed what would be. And more, it discerned what should be.

Scientific experts were thus not only the caretakers of the future, they were the guardians of Truth. They were a kind of superhuman elite—not at all unlike Plato's philosopher-kings—who ruled the untrained with a firm but beneficent hand in order to realize the high ideals of progress.

That meant that science had to necessarily be intermingled with ideology. It had to become an instrument of social transformation. It had to be harnessed with the idealism of the farsighted elite. It had to be wielded by the *cognoscenti* as a tool for the preordained task of human and cultural engineering. It had to be politicized.

Thus, in the early days of the twentieth century, science and millenarian politics were woven together into a crazy quilt of idealism, fanaticism, and ambition. It enabled a few powerful men and movements to believe the unbelievable, conceive the inconceivable, and imagine the unimaginable. According to philosopher Eric Voegelin, "This potent admixture of ideas and ideals became a kind of *le dernier cri*—the ideological craze of a new orthodoxy and the starry-eyed bludgeon of a new plutocracy."[23]

It was upon the foundations of this orthodox plutocracy that the enterprise of the modern centralized state was erected. And until those foundations crumbled under the weight of two world wars and a myriad of other twentieth-century horrors, the future that never happened was sustained by it as the future that almost was.

Question: Why do fascism, communism, and monopolistic capitalism all look the same? Answer: Because they are the same. They are all manifestations of trenchant ideological systems. Though one is a heresy of the right, one is a heresy of the left, and one is a heresy in the middle, all three concentrate power and money in the hands of a few at the expense of the many. All three ultimately mitigate against free markets, small family businesses, decentralized and diverse economies, and widely distributed private property ownership. In other words, all three are enemies of the American dream.

This awful modern notion is obviously a far cry from the kind of worldview the American founders and pioneers maintained. They shared a profound distrust of central governments to solve the grave problems that afflicted individuals, communities, and societies. Certainly they believed in a strong and active civil authority—but only in its proper place. Thus every brand of statist ideology was abhorred by them.

Thomas Jefferson warned against the danger of "reducing the society to the state or the state to society."[24] Likewise, Patrick Henry argued: "The contention that the civil government should at its option intrude into and exercise control over the family and the household is a great and pernicious error."[25]

Gouverneur Morris, the primary author of the first draft of the Constitution, insisted that the everyday affairs of society should be designed to avoid what he called the "interference of the state beyond its competence."[26]

Four Alternative Movements

This great conservative tradition was preserved in the first half of the twentieth century by four very distinctive—and for the most part independent—movements. Each has had a profound effect upon the thinking of Pat Buchanan. Each has contributed greatly to the pool of ideas he draws from as he formulates his contemporary populist campaign.

Though they seemed to come from the four ends of the earth temperamentally, philosophically, ecclesiastically, and geographically, all four movements had their genesis in a single year, 1891, and with a single purpose: to demonstrate genuine Christian compassion, justice, and mercy to all men everywhere; to model godly character to all the world.

In 1891, the versatile and prolific Abraham Kuyper—known to all the world as a preacher-turned-journalist-turned-politician in the Netherlands—delivered a sterling address to the first Christian Social Congress entitled *The Social Problem and the Christian Religion*. Though it spawned decades of healthy debate and constructive activity, its greatest contribution was to ignite the worldwide political phenomenon of the *Christian Democrat Movement*.

In 1891, the brilliant and pious Vincenzo Gioacchino Pecci—known to all the world as Leo XIII—issued the papal encyclical *Rerum Novarum*. It too spawned a decades-long resurgence of dynamic Catholic social policy. But like Kuyper's speech, the encyclical's greatest contribution was to give impetus to the international and ecumenical *Distributist Movement*.

In 1891, the energetic and irascible Alexander Lyle Stuart—known to all the world as a southern Confederate partisan-turned-gentleman book-binder—reprinted the works of the great statesman and political theorist John C. Calhoun with a brilliant and stirring introduction that called for a return to the underlying precepts of southern culture. Rallying around his ideas of property, family, and community, a whole new generation of Southern intellectuals regenerated the old notions of political decentralization and overlapping spheres of social authority—and thus gave rise to the *Southern Agrarian Movement*.

In 1891, the tireless and articulate Henry Cabot Lodge—known to all the world as an esteemed senator from the state of Massachusetts and a popular historical revisionist—delivered his most famous oration, entitled *Justice as the Fruit of Christian Diligence*. Delivered in Boston before luminaries assembled in celebration of the centennial of the Bill of Rights, the speech had an immediate short-term impact, but its long-term effect was to spawn the *American Progressive Movement*.

In 1891, a Dutch Calvinist, an Italian Catholic, a Southern Confederate, and a New England Caliban suddenly united—albeit unknowingly—to stand against the rising tide of ideology, to posit an all-encompassing worldview alternative, and to affirm with one voice the essential dynamic of the unencumbered Christian social ethic—the only substantial hopes for the disenfranchised and dispossessed in this poor fallen world. Distinctly anti-revolutionary, they stood on the firm foundation of old truths, long confirmed in the experience of men and the revelation of God.

Thus, as amazing as it may seem at first glance, each of the four great men—and each of the popular Christian resistance movements that they conceived—shared five essential presuppositions. Their astounding unanimity is nothing short of a brash witness to the superintending grace of a sovereign God. Whether Christian Democrat, Distributist, Southern Agrarian, or Progressive, these five principles remained fundamental to them all.

First, they shared a profound distrust of central governments to solve the grave problems that afflicted society, though each believed in a strong and active civil authority—but only in its proper place. Thus, every brand of statist ideology was abhorred by them. Kuyper quoted Jefferson, warning against the danger of "reducing the society to the state or the state to society."[27] Pope Leo likewise quoted Patrick Henry, arguing, "The contention that the civil government should at its option intrude into and exercise control over the family and the household is a great and pernicious error."[28] While Lodge insisted:

> Government is but a tool. If ever we come to the place where our tools determine what jobs we can or cannot do, and by what means, then nary a fortnight shall pass in which new freedoms shall be wrested from us straightway. Societal problems are solved by families and com-

munities as they carefully and discriminantly use a variety of tools.[29]

They believed social reform—like so much else in culture—should be designed to avoid what Leo called the "interference of the state beyond its competence."[30] C. S. Lewis, who was apparently influenced by at least three of these alternative movements, wrote: "Of all the tyrannies, a tyranny sincerely expressed for the good of its victims may be the most oppressive. It may be better to live under robber barons than under omnipotent ideological busybodies."[31]

Nowhere is the omnipotence of ideological busybodies more evident than in the social programs of the therapeutic and messianic state.

The *second* principle that the four movements shared was a deep and abiding commitment to widespread private property ownership. Each believed that if everyone within the society—rich and poor—were to be equipped and enabled over the long haul, they must be afforded the opportunity to own their own homes, tend their own gardens, and pass on an inheritance to their own children. This precluded all forms of egalitarianism, socialism, and welfarism—as well as the smothering tax structures necessary to support them. As Pope Leo said: "If one would undertake to alleviate the condition of the poor masses, the centrality and inviolability of private property must be established and protected."[32]

Similarly, Stuart asserted that:

Ownership of the means of production cannot be entrusted to socialistic bureaucrats any more than to monopolistic plutocrats. Three acres and a cow may seem hopelessly out of date as an answer to the cries of the needy—especially in light of the burden of taxation and regulation heaped upon the freeholds of our day. But the great lesson of history is clear enough: when men are left free to faithfully work at home, they are happiest and society is securest.[33]

True social security, they believed, was what Kuyper called the "broadest distribution of property through legitimate work as is humanly possible."[34]

The *third* principle that the four movements shared was a healthy understanding of human anthropology. They took into account the Fall. Thus, unlike the prevailing ideologies of the twentieth century, they expected no utopia, no quick fix, no magic wand, no ultimate solutions to the problems of social justice this side of eternity. They recognized the sway that greed, avarice, prejudice, and envy held in human affairs and thus acceded the need for private associations—guilds, unions, community organizations, fellowships, and fraternities—to maintain an appropriately decentralized checks and balances. According to Lodge:

Multiple jurisdictions and free associations are hedges against both tyranny and anarchy, against both cultural hegemony and civil disintegration. The medieval guilds were not collectivist but through communal means they enforced the necessity of upholding interpersonal responsibility and accountability—a profound Christian necessity in light of the deleterious effects of sin on men and man.[35]

Stuart concurred, saying:

There is a spiritual cancer at work in the world. The piracy of man's fallen nature invariably mitigates against freedom and justice. Therefore voluntary associations must needs balance us—without force of state but nonetheless with force of community—and hold us to accounts.[36]

Any successful program of social reform, they believed, would require what Pope Leo called the "cooperation of many and diverse elements within the community."[37]

The *fourth* principle that the four movements shared was an unwavering commitment to the family. Though they believed that private property was the best means for the poor to obtain a vehicle for change, and that voluntary associations girded that vehicle about with protection and integrity, the vehicle itself, they asserted, was the family.

Kuyper said: "According to the Word of God, the family is portrayed as the wonderful creation through which the rich fabric of our organic human life must spin itself out."[38]

Again he said, "The tasks of family in society lie outside government's jurisdiction. With those it is not to meddle."[39] Pope Leo called the family "the true society."[40] Lodge called it "the primary building block of our culture. Nay, it is itself our culture."[41] And Stuart called it "the only means by which real and substantial change for good might truly be effected."[42] They believed that culture must be family-centered if it is to be the least bit effective.

The *fifth* principle that the Christian Democrat, Distributist, Southern Agrarian, and Progressive movements shared was the certainty that the church was central to any and all efforts to mete out mercy, justice, and truth. They believed that while the family was the vehicle for substantive change, it was the church that drove that vehicle.

According to Kuyper:

Jesus set apart and sent out His church among the nations to influence society in three ways. The first and most important influence was through the ministry of the Word. . . . The church's second influence was through an organized ministry of charity. . . . Third, the church influenced society by instituting the equality of brotherhood—in contrast to differences in rank and station. . . . Indeed, as a direct consequence of Christ's appearing and the extension of His church among the nations, society has been remarkably changed.[43]

Pope Leo said, "No practical solutions to our problems will be found apart from the intervention of religion and of the church."[44] And again, "All the striving of men will be in vain if they leave out the church."[45]

Lodge concurred:

> Of all the institutions ordained of God upon this earth, this one has the force of integration: the church. We cannot hope to help the helpless apart from the church's ministrations of grace which transform the giver, the receiver, and even the gift itself.[46]

They believed that social reform should be, as Stuart said "guided, defined, managed, and provoked in, through, and by the church."[47]

Of all the precepts espoused by the Christian Democrat, Distributist, Southern Agrarian, and Progressive movements, it was this last one that most rankled the ire of twentieth-century ideologues. During the first half of this century, the church had already become the spurned and neglected stepchild of the modern era. It was perceived as being moss-backed and archaic. Or awkward and irrelevant.

And the church's reputation has only diminished with time. Today, it is regarded as little more than a water boy to the game of life. Sad, but all too true.

Part of the reason for this horribly low estimation of the church is due to the fact that the church has always *limped* through history. Men look at the all-too-evident, all-too-apparent, sometimes even glaring, weaknesses of Christ's Bride and just assume that its lame and crippled state is ample justification for dismissing its importance.

The fact is, though, the church's limp is actually a *confirmation* of its power, relevance, and significance.

After the Fall, God told Satan that the Righteous Deliverer, Jesus Christ, would crush his head. But God also said that, in the process, the heel of the Lord would be bruised (Gen. 3:15). The limp, then, that Christ's Body displays is actually a sign of great victory, not a sign of defeat or incompetence. It is an emblem of triumph.This reality is portrayed all throughout the Bible.

For instance, when Jacob, the father of Israel's twelve tribes, wrestled through the night at Peniel, he limped ever afterward as a sign that he had actually prevailed (Gen. 32:31).

The apostle Paul, father of the Gentile church, was given a thorn in the flesh. Since thorns grow along the ground, Paul was pricked—at least symbolically—in the foot. It kept him limping in the eyes of men (2 Cor. 12:7). Even so, it was in this weakness that Christ's power was affirmed and perfected (2 Cor. 12:9).

Thus, when the church limps through history, as believers we need not be frustrated or discouraged. On the contrary, we should be encouraged that God's Word is sure and true. For victory has, indeed, already been won.

The reality is that whatever the church does—or doesn't do—directly affects the course of civilization. It determines the flow of historical events (Rev. 5—6).

The church has the keys to the kingdom (Matt. 16:19). It has the power to bind and loose (Matt. 18:18). It has the authority to prevail over the very gates of hell (Matt. 16:18). It is, thus, the church—not governments or ideologies or systems or causes—that will determine our destiny and the destiny of our world.

The reason for this is threefold:

First, it is the church that offers us the source of life. It offers the waters of life (Rev. 22:17), the Bread of Life (John 6:32; 1 Cor. 11:24), and the Word of life (1 John 1:1). The sacramental ministry of the church is our *only* source for these grace provisions. There is nowhere else that we can turn for these "medicines of immortality." They effect a tangible offering to God, a consecration *before* God, a communion *with* God, and a transformation *in* God. Thus, they actually readjust us to the ultimate reality.

Second, the church offers us accountability and discipline. Sin cripples any work. Whenever sin is casually tolerated, all our efforts are defiled (1 Cor. 5:6–13), evangelism is stifled (1 Cor. 5:1–5), and victory is denied (Josh. 7:1–15). Only the church has the authority to discipline heinous sin (Matt. 18:15–20). The purpose of this kind of accountability is, of course, protective and restorative, not defensive or punitive. It is to erect a hedge of responsibility and respectability around our efforts to confront evil in this poor fallen world.

Third, the church offers us a place of rest. When as God's people we assemble ourselves together, we are at last able to lie down in green pastures, beside still water (Ps. 23:2). As we gather around the throne of grace, we are at last able to take refuge and find sanctuary (Ps. 61:1–4). We are able to enter His gates with thanksgiving and His courts with praise (Ps. 100:4).

Without the context of the church, even the most dynamic political and social economy is exposed to atrophy and entropy. But, within that context, we have an unprecedented opportunity to attain glorious heights—even as we limp along the battlefield of this culture.

A lack of confidence in the state, a reliance on private property, a realistic anthropology, a reliance upon the family, and a subsuming trust in the church: These five principles drove—and to whatever degree they still exist, still drive—the Christian Democrat, Distributist, Southern Agrarian, and Progressive movements.

In fact, they represent the only serious dissent from the failed ideologies of the twentieth century. Together they comprise an altogether alternate sociology—one that was repudiated by the powers and principalities but not by providence. Together they are "a perpetually defeated thing which survives all its conquerors."[48] So said the great Distributist writer, G. K. Chesterton.

In the end, we must say along with Titus and the apostle Paul, "These things are good and profitable to men" (Titus 3:8).

Certainly, that has been the opinion of Pat Buchanan as he has taken up the themes of each of these movements in turn throughout his career.

The Cataclysm of 1912

Of course, Buchanan is not the first intellectual/politician to take up the themes of the Christian Democrat, Distributist, Southern Agrarian, and Progressive movements. The Christian Democrat Abraham Kuyper eventually became prime minister of the Netherlands. The Distributist Hilaire Belloc served a term in the English Parliament. The Southern Agrarian J. Evetts Haley was influential in Texas politics all his life. But perhaps the greatest of these peculiar conservatives was the Progressive Theodore Roosevelt.

Before his fiftieth birthday he had served as a New York State legislator, the under-secretary of the Navy, police commissioner for the City of New York, U.S. Civil Service commissioner, the governor of the State of New York, the vice president under William McKinley, a colonel in the U.S. Army, and two terms as the president of the United States. In addition, he had run a cattle ranch in the Dakota Territories, served as a reporter and editor for several journals, newspapers, and magazines, and conducted scientific expeditions on four continents. He read at least five books every week of his life and wrote nearly sixty on an astonishing array of subjects— from history and biography to natural science and social criticism. He enjoyed hunting, boxing, and wrestling. He was an amateur taxidermist, botanist, ornithologist, and astronomer. He was a devoted family man who lovingly raised five children. And he enjoyed a lifelong romance with his wife.

But of all his adventures and accomplishments, his involvement in the presidential race of 1912 was perhaps the most significant—and certainly, the most controversial. That year, the electorate was confounded by a whole host of damning dilemmas.

William Taft, the Republican incumbent, was the uninspiring successor to Roosevelt—who was unquestionably one of the most popular presidents in American history. He was a decent man; there was no disputing that. But he seemed to lack vision. Though he had a brilliant legal mind and vast foreign policy experience, he appeared to be bland and inarticulate. He seemed to have no ideas of his own—and even those that he did have seemed terribly muddled. By all appearances he epitomized an entrenched and institutional politics-as-usual.

His fiery Democratic opponent was Woodrow Wilson. Though he had served briefly—and without distinction—as governor of New Jersey, he was essentially a political unknown. And yet because the campaign hinged on the whole issue of change, anything seemed possible.

According to Wilson, change was essential. "Our life has broken away from the past," he said.[49] "Old political formulas do not fit the present problems."[50] He believed, "This is nothing short of a new social age, a new era of human relationships, a new stage setting for the drama of life."[51]

Wilson was convinced that the "new age"[52] demanded "new circumstances"[53] and the "fitting of a new social organization."[54]

He wanted to "bring the government back to the people"[55] through an aggressive implementation of activist legislation, adjudication, and administration. He advocated radical change: "Politics in America is a case which sadly requires attention. The system set up by our law and our usage doesn't work—or at least it cannot be depended on."[56]

Wilson boasted that we ought to reinvent the world by "interpreting the Constitution according to the Darwinian principle"[57] and by becoming "architects in our time."[58] He foresaw the advent of "a glorious New World Order"[59] and "a marvelous New Freedom."[60]

Because Taft seemed either unwilling or unable to deflect Wilson's energetic barrage of ideological rhetoric, Theodore Roosevelt reluctantly came out of retirement and took to the stump. He decried the liberalism of Wilson, saying that the nation should be "ruled by the Ten Commandments"[61] not "by Darwinian presumption."[62] He claimed that "the great heart of the nation beats for truth, honor, and liberty,"[63] and thus he felt compelled to decry "the immorality and absurdity" of Wilson's "doctrines of socialism."[64] He asserted that he was an "old school conservative" who believed in "the progressive notions" that made for "a strong people and a tame government."[65]

Taft was chagrined. He fought back with a derisive negative campaign. He accused his old friend Roosevelt of "reckless ambition."[66] He chided his old boss of "unsettling of the fundamentals of our government"[67] and called him a "serious menace and an extremist."[68]

Though Roosevelt handily won the hearts of the grass roots and secured nine out of every ten electable delegates sent to the national convention, he was eventually denied the Republican nomination through a series of

last-minute backroom maneuvers by the party establishment. Scandalized and demoralized, the Republicans divided—the "moderates" stood by Taft while the "pro-
gressives" remained loyal to Roosevelt.

The politics-as-usual finagling, mudslinging, and con-
niving outraged the popular press and exacerbated the
electorate. Disaffection with the entire process ran ram-
pant. Roosevelt angrily charged:

> The old parties are husks, with no real soul within either,
> divided on artificial lines, boss ridden and privilege con-
> trolled, each a jumble of incongruous elements and nei-
> ther daring to speak out wisely and fearlessly what should
> be said on the vital issues of the day.[69]

As the campaign progressed, it appeared that his last-
minute, third-party challenge might actually defy all
odds and succeed. But then, with less than three weeks
to go, Roosevelt was the victim of an assassination attempt. Though his wound was not mortal, he was unable to return to the rigors of the campaign. Uncertainty
suddenly gripped the electorate.

On election day, ambivalence reigned. None of the
candidates received a majority. Though Wilson attained
a weak plurality and was declared the winner, slightly
more than 57 percent of the popular vote went against
him. As a result, he entered the White House the next
year without any semblance of a mandate, facing a for-
midable array of opposition forces.

Though he acted decisively to implement his radical

agenda—four constitutional amendments were passed that revolutionized the nature of American governance—and he was able to concentrate vast new powers in the hands of the central government, Wilson was never able to win popular support. He somehow survived a tepid reelection bid—but again without a majority and with only lethargic participation by eligible voters.

By the end of that second term, the whole conception of activist government had been thoroughly repudiated. Wilson was mired in scandalous unpopularity. His administration was a disaster. The world was in shambles following the Great War. And the peace of Versailles portended even worse. Democracy had done all that Socialism had threatened to do.

The electorate realized that it must rally from its dismal and equivocal funk. Thankfully, it did.

Warren G. Harding, the conservative Republican candidate, issued a clarion call for a return to "normalcy." He said:

> America's present need is not heroics, but healing; not nostrums, but normalcy; not revolution, but restoration; not agitation, but adjustment; not surgery, but serenity. The world needs to be reminded that all human ills are not curable by legislation, and that quantity of statutory enactment and excess of government offer no substitute for quality of citizenship.[70]

America was ready for a return to the quiet certainty that while politics is important, it is not all-important.

Voters had to get past their natural reticence and ambivalence. They realized that sometimes political involvement must take precedence in our lives in order to ensure that political involvement does not take preeminence over our lives. They had learned that lesson the hard way.

They gave Harding a landslide victory. Ultimately though, it was a victory for Roosevelt—the platform the Republicans ran on was virtually identical to the one he had espoused just a few years prior. It consisted of a kind of "new conservatism of the heart."

History does not repeat itself. Every step along the way in mankind's inevitable march toward eternity is individual and unique. But there are moments when the resemblances are uncanny.

Buchanan may well be the Roosevelt of our time.

Let us pray that we would recognize those resemblances before we are forced to—by the dumb certainties of experience.

PART III

Tomorrow's Mainstream

The foes of our own household are our worst enemies; and we can oppose them, not only by exposing them and denouncing them, but by constructive work in planning and building reforms which shall take into account both the economic and the moral factors in human advance. We in America can attain our great destiny only by service; not by rhetoric, and above all not by insincere rhetoric, and that dreadful mental double-dealing and verbal juggling which makes promises and repudiates them, and says one thing at one time, and the directly opposite thing at another time. Our service must be the service of deeds.

—*Theodore Roosevelt*[1]

CHAPTER 6

The Last Hurrah

*The important thing generally is the next step. We ought
not to take it unless we are sure that it is advisable; but
we should not hesitate to take it once we are sure; and
we can safely join with others who also wish to take it,
without bothering our heads overmuch as to any
somewhat fantastic theories they may have concerning,
say, the two hundredth step, which is not yet in sight.*

—*Theodore Roosevelt*[2]

According to columnist James Braden, the populist movement of Patrick Buchanan "may not be the
campaign of the present, but it most assuredly is the
campaign of the future." It represents, he says, a paradigm shift in American politics:

Because it represents the integrated interests of the people in both economic security and moral stability, it is a
campaign that simply will not go away. It is a campaign
that will produce profound effects in the American political landscape for generations to come. It would not be
too much to say that in losing the nomination to Bob
Dole, Pat Buchanan has kept alive the hopes and dreams

of the Founding Fathers in a new and profound way. If nothing else, this one contribution of his new conservatism of the heart will have made all the effort worth it.[3]

If that is true, then the Buchanan campaign is a harbinger of a substantial amount of political activity and reform in the future. Interestingly, as novel as this notion seems, it has rather antiquarian roots—roots in the soil of the Old American Order.

In a very real sense, Buchanan has brought us "back to the future."

The great experiment in liberty we enjoy in America was a deliberate attempt to establish a conservative order of stability, justice, and honor. The tremendous freedoms that we exercise were thus carefully secured against the arbitrary and fickle whims of men and movements by the rule of law. Our social system was not designed so as to depend upon the benevolence of the magistrates, or the altruism of the wealthy, or the condescension of the powerful. Every citizen, rich or poor, man or woman, native-born or immigrant, hale or handicapped, young or old, is equal under the standard of unchanging, immutable, and impartial justice.

As Thomas Paine wrote in *Common Sense,* the powerful booklet that helped spark the War for Independence, "In America, the law is king."[4]

If left to the mere discretion of human authorities, even the best-intended statutes, edicts, and ordinances inevitably devolve into some form of death-dealing tyranny. There must, therefore, be an absolute against which no encroachment of prejudice or preference may interfere. There must be a foundation that the winds of change and the waters of circumstance cannot erode. There must be a basis for law that can be depended upon at all times, in all places, and in every situation.

Apart from this uniquely Christian innovation in the affairs of men and nations, there can be no freedom. There never has been before, and there never will be again. Our Founding Fathers knew that only too well.

The opening refrain of the *Declaration of Independence* affirms the necessity of that kind of absolute standard upon which the rule of law can then be established:

> We hold these truths to be self-evident, that all men are created equal; that they are endowed by their Creator with certain inalienable rights; that among these are life, liberty, and the pursuit of happiness. That, to secure these rights, governments are instituted among men, deriving their just powers from the consent of the governed.[5]

Appealing to the "Supreme Judge of the World" for guidance, and relying on His "Divine Providence" for wisdom, the framers committed themselves and their posterity to the absolute standard of "the laws of nature and of nature's God."[6] A just government exists, they argued, solely and completely to "provide guards" for the "future security" of that standard.[7] Take away those guards, and the rule of law is no longer possible.

G. K. Chesterton once quipped that "America is the

only nation in the world that is founded on a creed."[8] Other nations find their identity and cohesion in ethnicity, or geography, or cultural tradition. But America was founded on certain ideas—about freedom, about human dignity, about social responsibility. It was this profound peculiarity that most struck Alexis de Tocqueville during his famous visit to this land at the beginning of the nineteenth century. He called it "American exceptionalism."

In essence, this is the core of the message of Patrick Buchanan's populist campaign—of his "new conservatism of the heart." Whether on the stump, in print, over the airwaves, or in animated one-on-one conversation, he is likely to remind his listeners that America's special blessings are the result of generations-long adherence to this special creed—America's exceptionalism is the legacy of principled men and women who were willing to give their all in all that we might be able to enjoy the benefits of the covenant.

It was this exceptional sort of creedalism that animated the Founding Fathers—and caused them to so boldly declare their autonomy from the British realm. The activist government of the Crown had become increasingly intrusive, burdensome, and fickle and thus the possibility of rule of law had been thrown into very real jeopardy. The Founders merely protested the fashion and fancy of political, bureaucratic, and systemic innovation that had alienated those things which ought to ever be inalienable.

They said that the king's government had "erected a multitude of new offices, and sent hither swarms of of-

ficers to harass our people, and eat out their substance."[9] It had "called together legislative bodies at
places unusual, uncomfortable, and distant . . . for the
sole purpose of fatiguing them into compliance with the
King's measures."[10] It had "refused assent to laws, the
most wholesome and necessary to the public good."[11] It
had "imposed taxes without consent . . . taking away
our charters, abolishing our most valuable laws, and al-
tering fundamentally the forms of our government."[12]
And it had "plundered our seas, ravaged our coasts, destroyed the lives of our people . . . and excited domestic insurrections amongst us."[13]

In short, their society had devolved to the ancient de-
crepitudes of tyranny. And that was, to their minds, an
intolerable reversion that must be rectified at any and all
costs.

The Founders believed that no one in America could
be absolutely secure under the king, because absolute-
ness had been thrown out of the constitutional vocabu-
lary. Because certain rights had been abrogated for at
least some citizens by a smothering, dominating political
behemoth, all of the liberties of all the citizens were at
risk because suddenly arbitrariness, relativism, and ran-
domness had entered into the legal equation. The checks
against petty partiality and blatant bias had been virtually
disabled.

Thus, they acted boldly to "form a more perfect
union."[14] They launched a sublime experiment in liberty
never before surpassed, never again matched—one

rooted in the biblical principles and precepts of the inalienable: "life, liberty, and the pursuit of happiness."

From Life to Liberty

The Founders recognized that all human freedom
must begin by breaking the old pagan shackles of death
and destruction by affirming the fundamental right to
life. They also knew that they could only affirm it—they
could not give it, because it was not theirs to give.

Life is God's gift. It is His gracious endowment upon
the created order. It flows forth in generative fruitful-
ness. The American Founders recognized that this great
Christian legacy of life was the foundation upon which
all other freedoms must necessarily be built. In order to
establish liberty and justice for all they must first affirm
the right to life for all. Everything else flowed from that
fundamental tenant.

Thus, Thomas Jefferson asserted that "the chief purpose of government is to protect life. Abandon that and
you have abandoned all."[15]

Historian Harold Lane has said:

The Framers of the American system drew deeply from
the wells of human experience—they were learned men
who had a firm grasp of the flow of history and the consequence of particular ideas. Whether or not they were
personally pious, they knew the Christian tradition afforded them the only substantial hope of breaking the
ancient strangle-hold of tyranny on men and nations.

They chose as the cornerstone of their nascent experiment a profound respect for life, for they believed such a principled perspective was the very essence of their redemptive religion. Without it, all else would ultimately prove to be futile—regardless of how noble the notions might be.[16]

Understanding this, Abraham Lincoln pressed home the same issue when he questioned the institution of chattel slavery on the basis of the sanctity of all human life and the rule of law:

> I should like to know if taking this old *Declaration of Independence,* which declares that all men are equal upon principle, and making exceptions to it, where it will stop. If one man says it does not mean a Negro, why not another say it does not mean some other man?[17]

Liberty is a deeply ingrained biblical conception. The message of the gospel is a proclamation of "liberty to the captives" (Luke 4:18 ASV). It sets men free (John 8:32). We are set free from the condemnation of sin (Rom. 8:1), from the bondage of the flesh (1 Peter 2:16), and from the oppression of lawlessness (James 1:25). "It was for freedom that Christ set us free" (Gal. 5:1 ASV). "If therefore, the Son shall make you free, you shall be free indeed" (John 8:36 ASV). We can "walk in liberty" (Ps. 119:45) for "where the Spirit of the Lord is, there is liberty" (2 Cor. 3:17).

The American Founders translated this central concern for spiritual freedom to every other arena under the lordship of Christ—including the arena of politics and culture. They saw in the gospel a spiritual emphasis on freedom that they believed could—and even should—be applied to the temporal realm no less passionately. It was not merely high-sounding rhetoric that prompted Patrick Henry to declare "Give me liberty or give me death."[18] It was a careful formulation of his theology—a theology that ran far back into the nether traditions of Christendom.

He and his fellow patriots realized that freedom relies on the prior subjugation of the precepts of the Fall (Col. 2:13–15). Liberty cannot be had apart from an affirmation of the sanctity of life and a condemnation of the tyranny of death. One or the other must prevail.

Similarly, the pursuit of happiness is a biblical ideal. It is a theme that resounds throughout the poetic literature of Scripture (Ps. 36:8; 40:8; 133:1) as well as the wisdom literature (Prov. 3:13; 14:21; 16:20; 29:18). In the great manifesto of His kingdom, the Sermon on the Mount, Jesus identified blessedness or happiness as the most characteristic and distinguishing mark of true spirituality and humble righteousness (Matt. 5:3–10).

But again, this providential endowment is beyond the pale of human experience apart from the prior subjugation of sin and death (1 Cor. 15:19–21). When Thomas Jefferson chose the familiar phrase "life, liberty, and the pursuit of happiness" instead of the more traditional formulation of his intellectual mentor John Locke, "life, liberty, and property," he too was deliberately affirming a dogmatic continuity between the old Christian consensus and the new American experiment. Apart from the hope of those gospel principles, he and his fellow patriots saw no other alternative than the dystopic degradation of pagan barbarism, oppression, and tyranny.

A Cultural Caveat

According to author P. J. O'Rourke:

> There are twenty-seven specific complaints against the British Crown set forth in the Declaration of Independence. To modern ears they still sound reasonable. They still sound reasonable in large part, because so many of them can be leveled against the present federal government of the United States.[19]

For many, the realization that somehow our Founders' unique experiment in liberty has gone off the rails is a fairly recent revelation. But there have been others with much greater prescience.

In 1930 an extraordinary group of Southern historians, poets, political scientists, novelists, and journalists published a prophetic collection of essays warning against the looming loss of the Founding Fathers' original vision. Including contributions from such literary luminaries as Robert Penn Warren, Donald Davidson, Allen Tate, Andrew Nelson Lytle, Stark Young, and John Crowe Ransom, the symposium—entitled *I'll Take My Stand*—poignantly voiced the complex intellectual, emotional, and spiritual consternation of men standing on the precipice of catastrophic cultural change.

The men were alarmed by what they perceived to be a steady erosion of the rule of law in modern American life. They feared that—as was the case in the eighteenth century—our liberties were facing a fearsome challenge from the almost omnipresent and omnipotent forces of monolithic government. They said:

> When we remember the high expectations held univer-sally by the founders of the American union for a more perfect order of society, and then consider the state of life in this country today, it is bound to appear to reason-able people that somehow the experiment has very nearly proved abortive, and that in some way a great common-wealth has gone wrong.[20]

They were determined to warn against the creeping dehumanization of an ideological secularism that they believed was already beginning to dominate American life:

> There is evidently a kind of thinking that rejoices in set-ting up a social objective which has no relation to the individual. Men are prepared to sacrifice their private dignity and happiness to an abstract social ideal, and without asking whether the social ideal produces the wel-fare of any individual man whatsoever.[21]

They knew full well that they were essentially standing against the rising tide of industrial modernity, nevertheless, they were convinced that ordinary Americans would ultimately hear and heed their warning—otherwise, the nation would collapse under the weight of corruption:

> If the republic is to live up to its ideals and be what it could be, then it had better look long and hard at what it is in danger of becoming and devote conscious effort to controlling its own destiny, rather than continuing to drift along on the tides of economic materialism.[22]

Clearly, the contributors were old-line conservatives in the tradition of Americans like John Adams, Fisher Ames, John Randolph, and John Calhoun. But they also drew on the rich European conservative tradition of men like Edmund Burke, Walter Bagehot, Robert Southey, and Thomas Macaulay. They were heirs themselves of the four alternative movements—Christian Democrat, Distributist, Southern Agrarian, and Progressive—that so dominated alternative political thought in their time. As political scientist Louis Rubin later commented:

> They were writing squarely out of an old American tradition, one that we find embedded in American thought almost from the earliest days. The tradition was that of the pastoral; they were invoking the humane virtues of a simpler, more elemental, non-acquisitive existence, as a needed rebuke to the acquisitive, essentially materialistic compulsions of a society that from the outset was very much engaged in seeking wealth, power, and plenty on a continent whose prolific natural resources and vast acres

of usable land, forests, and rivers were there for the tak-ing.[23]

Short-term pessimists but long-term optimists, they believed that eventually a grass-roots movement would restore the principles of the rule of law and that the American dream could be preserved for future genera-tions. Though they were not economists or sociologists or activists, their vision was a comprehensive blueprint for a genuinely principle-based conservative renewal.

Thus, they believed in an extremely limited form of government and took a dim view of government inter-vention. They went so far as to assert that communities should "ask practically nothing of the federal govern-ment in domestic legislation."[24] Further, they believed that this limited governmental structure should be pred-icated primarily on the tenets of "local self-government" and "decentralization."[25]

They were not minimalists or libertarians. Instead they were realists who envisioned a society that called "only for enough government to prevent men from injuring one another."[26] It was, by its very nature, a "non-ideo-logical" and "*laissez faire* society."[27] It was an "individ-ualistic society" that "only asked to be let alone."[28]

Not surprisingly then, the contributors to the sympo-sium opposed the idea that "the government should set up an economic super organization, which in turn would become the government."[29] They regarded Socialism, Democratic Liberalism, Communism, and Republican Cooperationism with equal disdain.[30] In fact, they professed an ingrained "suspicion of all schemes that propose to coerce our people to their alleged benefit."[31] They were, at heart, opposed to all manner of Utopianism—whether of the left or the right.

They believed that it was necessary "to employ a certain skepticism even at the expense of the Cult of Science, and to say it is an Americanism, which looks innocent and disinterested, but really is not either."[32] They were not resistant to technological progress so much as they were resistant to the crass and inhuman humanism that often accompanies industrial advance. They believed that "a way of life that omits or de-emphasizes the more spiritual side of existence is necessarily disastrous to all phases of life."[33]

Clearly then, the men who contributed to *I'll Take My Stand* believed that society ought to be defined by its moral and cultural values. They yearned for return to that early American ethic of freedom and liberty, which was "for the most part stable, religious, and agrarian; where the goodness of life was measured by a scale of values having little to do with material values."[34]

In essence, they believed in humanizing the scale of modern life: "restoring such practices as manners, conversation, hospitality, sympathy, family life, romantic love—the social exchanges which reveal and develop sensibility in human affairs."[35] They believed in a "realistic, stable, and hereditable life."[36] Thus, they favored continuity and tradition over change for the sake of change: "The past is always a rebuke to the present; it's a better rebuke than any dream of the future. It's a better rebuke because you can see what some of the costs were, what frail virtues were achieved in the past by frail men."[37]

After all, they said: "Affections, and long memories, attach to the ancient bowers of life in the provinces; but they will not attach to what is always changing."[38]

Although they believed that all of these foundational truths were "self-evident" in the sense that they are written on the fleshly tablet of every man's heart, they were not so idealistic as to believe that the truths would be universally accepted.[39] In fact, they knew that such reasoning would inevitably be a stumbling block to some and mere foolishness to others.[40] All too often men suppress reality in one way, shape, form, or another.

As a matter of fact, though *I'll Take My Stand* caused quite a stir when it was first released, very few critics gave it much chance of actually affecting the course of events or the destiny of the nation. It was assumed that "the wheels of progress could not possibly be redirected."[41] The contributors were chided for their "naiveté," "impracticality," and "wistfulness."[42] They were written off as "merely nostalgic," "hopelessly idealistic," and "enthusiasts for an epochal past that can never again be recaptured."[43]

For some fifty years it looked as if the critics might be right. The course of the twentieth century appeared to be a stern rebuke to the basic principles of the symposium. The devotees of the twentieth century's ideological worldview seemed to have won the day and supplanted the old Christian consensus of life, liberty, and the pursuit of happiness. Like the English Distributists and the Continental Christian Democrats, with whom they shared so many basic presuppositions, the contributors looked tragically out of step with the times. Now, though, it seems as if the utopian social planners of Planned Parenthood are the ones who are cast out of favor as "hopelessly idealistic."

Everything has changed. Recent turns of events have vindicated the realists' emphasis on the founding vision of the American Republic: less government, lower taxes, family values, minimal regulation, localism, and the distinctive Christian virtues of life, liberty, and the pursuit of happiness. Their innate distrust of professional politicians, propagandizing media, and commercial tomfoolery have suddenly been translated by a spontaneous grass-roots advent into populist megatrends. The fulfillment of their improbable prophetic caveat is even now unfolding as we race toward the end of the century.

What Plays in Peoria

What plays in Peoria these days is a distinctly conservative message of life, liberty, and the pursuit of happiness. Though you might have never known it from the way the dominant media reports on the current cultural trends, a tidal wave of conservative sentiment has already begun to sweep across the nation. Whether in local or national affairs, Americans are showing their impatience with the meddling social planners who have created our current designer disaster. In race after race and in instance after instance, voters have stunned the experts by resorting to the values and the principles of a supposedly bygone era.

It is not mere "anger with Washington" or "a temperamental hankering for change" that has driven this cultural revolution. Americans have awakened from a long slumber only to discover that their most precious freedoms are in jeopardy. They have thus sent a clear signal: The tired nostrums of utopian politics-as-usual simply will not suffice in the days ahead.

Surveys following the last two rounds of elections found that more than 54 percent of all Americans want "less government and less taxes."[44] A full 68 percent would prefer "a government that encouraged traditional values."[45] Nearly 87 percent favor legal restrictions on abortion-on-demand. An overwhelming 89 percent oppose relaxing the behavioral restrictions on homosexuals in the military.[46] And some 62 percent oppose conferring on them preferential minority status.[47]

When asked to identify the most important issues facing the nation today, "reducing taxes and government spending" was selected by more than a two-to-one ratio over any other concern.[48] But surprisingly, "reinforcing traditional family values" came in next, followed by "prohibiting abortion," "promoting freedom and democracy," and "eliminating government regulations."[49]

Despite strong opposition by the entire politics-as-usual establishment, term-limit proposals won in all fourteen states where they have appeared on the ballot.[50] In thirteen of those states—including California, Michigan, Missouri, Ohio, and Florida—they won decisively, taking an average of 66 percent of the vote.[51] The only close vote was in Washington state, where opponents launched a lavish media barrage against the proposal, and it still won with 52 percent.[52] Statewide tax increase measures lost in every single instance around the country while local tax increases and bond issues lost in 97 percent of the ballot measures coast to coast.[53]

Conservative candidates running pro-life and pro-family campaigns have "won hundreds of races" during the last two election cycles "at state and local levels, establishing themselves as a grassroots political force."[54] In fact, explicitly Christian candidates have won in about 40 percent of all the races nationwide.[55]

Given these remarkable turnarounds, it is hardly surprising to find that American voters who identified themselves as conservatives outnumbered self-identified liberals by a nine-to-five ratio.[56]

The moral principles that seemed so passé just a short time ago now actually dominate the social scene. The notions espoused by the contributors to *I'll Take My Stand* have gone from the cultural backwater to the political mainstream almost overnight. A kind of American *glasnost* and *perestroika* are beginning to have their effect on the entrenched structures of ideological power.

A new day has dawned. And it is not just "a natural swing of the politic pendulum" as some would have us believe.[57]

Senator Ted Kennedy recently asserted that "the ballot box is the place where change begins in America."[58] Although he has been fiercely and vehemently wrong in the past, Kennedy has never been more wrong than this. As George Will has argued: "There is hardly a page of American history that does not refute that insistence, so characteristic of the political class, on the primacy of politics in the making of history."[59]

In fact, he says, "In a good society, politics is peripheral to much of the pulsing life of the society."[60]

That is what makes the emergence of the conservative consensus such a threat to the politics-as-usual agenda of career politicians.[61] That is why their advocates in the dominant media recoil with fear and loathing when twenty million listeners tune in daily to Rush Limbaugh, Marlin Maddoux, David Gold, Wes Minter, Randall Terry, and other conservative talk-radio hosts.[62] That is why the pundits, the prognosticators, and the politicos are so terribly out of sorts just now.[63]

And it is why they react so violently to the populist campaign of Pat Buchanan.

They are suddenly discovering that the brutal imposition of fashion and fancy by a few privileged interlopers makes for an inherently unstable societal structure—one that is certain to be short-lived. They are discovering that Americans are not yet ready to surrender their inalienable rights to life, liberty, and the pursuit of happiness.

What the political establishment and its cohorts are witnessing—to their obvious horror—is the implementation of an extraordinary conservative strategy for the restoration of our republic: a return to those things that matter most. What they are witnessing is a return to common sense by common folk.

What they are witnessing is nothing less than the future.

It is the great lesson of history that ordinary people are ultimately the ones who determine the outcome of human events—not kings and princes, not masters and tyrants. It is laborers and workmen, cousins and acquaintances that upend the expectations of the brilliant and the glamorous, the expert and the meticulous. It is plain folks, simple people, who literally change the course of history—because they are the stuff of which history is made. They are the ones who make the world go round. For, as G. K. Chesterton said, "The most extraordinary thing in the world is an ordinary man and an ordinary woman and their ordinary children."[64]

Ultimately, that is the essence of the restoration of hope in this land—and the simultaneous obsolescence of the establishment's politics-as-usual utopian dream. It is simply a new grass-roots majoritarian emphasis on things that really matter: hearth and home, community and culture, accountability and availability, service and substance, morality and magnanimity, responsibility and restoration, life and liberty. Those things that may be subverted, stymied, obstructed, and hampered—but ultimately they cannot be obliterated.

What we are witnessing in the election of 1996 may very well be—as Pat Buchanan has asserted—the last hurrah of the establishment. The sounds coming from over the hill are not the clanging of the pitchforks—it is the death rattle of the knights and nobles.

As the famed journalist H. L. Mencken once said: "The man who invents a new imbecility is hailed gladly, and bidden to make himself at home; he is to the great masses of men, the beau ideal of mankind. His madness must necessarily give way to right, sooner or later, though—usually later."[65]

Or as the poet F. W. Faber wrote: "For right is right, since God is God, / And right the day must win; / To doubt would be disloyalty, / To falter would be sin."[66]

Notes

ACKNOWLEDGMENTS

[1] Theodore Roosevelt, *The Foes of Our Own Household* (New York: Charles Scribner's Sons, 1926), 149.

[2] Lyman Abbot, ed., *A Guide to Reading* (New York: Doubleday, 1917), 120.

INTRODUCTION

[1] Maurice Garland Fulton, ed., *Roosevelt's Writings* (New York: Macmillan, 1922), 36.

[2] *Atlantic Monthly,* February 1996.

[3] Ibid.

[4] Ibid.

[5] *Weekly Standard,* March 11, 1996.

[6] *Newsweek,* March 4, 1996.

[7] *New York Times,* February 25, 1996.

[8] *U.S. News and World Report,* February 26, 1996.

[9] *The New Yorker,* March 25, 1996.

[10] *The Tennessean,* February 28, 1996.

[11] *Wall Street Journal,* March 6, 1996.

[12] *Washington Post,* February 21, 1996.

[13] *The Wanderer,* February 29, 1996.

[14] *Weekly Standard,* March 11, 1996.

[15] *Associated Press,* February 26, 1996.

[16] *Time,* March 4, 1996.

[17] James Fenimore Cooper, *The American Democrat* (New York: Knopf, 1931), vii.

[18] Ibid.

PART I/CHAPTER 1

[1] Thomas H. Russell, ed., *Life and Work of Theodore Roosevelt* (New York: L. H. Walter), 257.

[2] Fulton, ed., *Roosevelt's Writings,* 166.

[3] *The Wanderer,* February 29, 1996.

[4] *New Yorker,* March 25, 1996.

[5] *New American,* March 18, 1996.

[6] Ibid.

[7] Ibid.

[8] Ibid.

[9] *World,* March 9, 1996.

[10] Ibid.

[11] *U.S. News and World Report,* March 4, 1996.

[12] *New York Times,* March 13, 1996.

[13] *World,* March 11, 1996.

[14] *Time,* March 4, 1996.

[15] *Weekly Standard,* March 11, 1996.

[16] *Nashville Banner,* February 23, 1996.

[17] *New American,* March 18, 1996.

[18] Ibid.

[19] *Newsweek,* March 4, 1996.

[20] *Time,* November 6, 1995.

[21] Ibid.

[22] *New York Outlook,* March 20, 1996.

[23] Ibid.

[24] *The Economist,* February 24, 1996.

[25] George Bernard Shaw, *Pygmalion* (New York: Signet Classic, 1969), 37.

[26] *The Howard Phillips Issues and Strategies Bulletin,* November 30, 1994.

[27] Hilaire Belloc, *Charles the First* (Philadelphia: Lippincott, 1933), 22.

[28] William J. Bennett, *The Index of Leading Cultural Indicators* (New York: Simon & Schuster, 1994), 8.

[29] Ibid.

[30] Ibid., i.

[31] Ibid.

[32] Ibid.

[33] Ibid.

[34] Arthur Schlessinger, *The Disuniting of America* (New York: Simon & Schuster, 1993).

[35] Daniel Patrick Moynihan, *Pandaemonium* (New York: Oxford, 1993).

[36] Bennett, *Leading Cultural Indicators,* 10.

[37] Ibid.

[38] Ibid.

39 *BBC Report,* November 2, 1980.

40 Zbigniew Brzezinski, *Out of Control* (New York: Scribners, 1993).

41 *Forbes,* September 14, 1992.

42 Charles Colson, *Against the Night* (Ann Arbor, Mich.: Servant, 1989), 19.

43 George Grant, *The Family Under Siege* (Minneapolis: Bethany House, 1994).

44 George Grant and Mark Horne, *Legislating Immorality* (Chicago: Moody Press, 1993).

45 George Grant, *The 57% Solution* (Franklin, Tenn.: Adroit Press, 1993).

46 George Barna, *Absolute Confusion* (Ventura, Calif.: Regal, 1993).

47 Os Guinness, *The American Hour* (New York: Free Press, 1992), 4.

48 *Forbes,* September 14, 1992.

49 Ibid.

50 Ibid.

51 Samuel Fallows, *The American Manual and Patriot Handbook* (Chicago: Century, 1888), 18.

52 E. J. Dionne, *Why Americans Hate Politics* (New York: Simon & Schuster, 1991), 9–11.

53 G. K. Chesterton, *G. F. Watts* (New York: E. P. Dutton and Co., 1901), 1.

54 *Washington Post,* July 5, 1990.

55 Jon Winokur, *The Portable Curmudgeon* (New York: Penguin, 1987), 220.

56 Alexis de Tocqueville, *The Republic of the United States of America: Its Political Institutions Reviewed and Examined, Vol. 1* (New York: A. S. Barnes, 1856), 275.

57 Winokur, *The Portable Curmudgeon,* 220.

58 Dionne, *Why Americans Hate Politics,* 9.

59 Ibid., 18.

60 *Remnant Review,* November 6, 1992.

61 A. James Reichley, *The Life of the Parties: A History of American Political Parties* (New York: Free Press, 1992).

62 Michael Drummond, *Participatory Democracy: A New Federalism in the Making* (New York: L. T. Carnell and Sons, 1923), 19.

63 Ibid., 22.

64 Ralph Ketcham, *The Anti-Federalist Papers* (New York: Mentor, 1986).

65 Drummond, *Participatory Democracy,* 17.

[66] Ross Lence, *Union and Liberty: The Political Philosophy of John C. Calhoon* (Indianapolis, Ind.: Liberty Press, 1992).

[67] Frances Fox Piven and Richard A. Cloward, *Why Americans Don't Vote* (New York: Pantheon, 1988), 5.

[68] Ibid., 19.

[69] Ibid., 122.

[70] Ibid., 54.

[71] *USA Today,* November 4, 1992.

[72] *Nashville Banner,* November 4, 1992.

[73] *Time,* November 16, 1992.

[74] *Augusta Picayune,* November 5, 1992.

[75] *New American,* March 18, 1996.

[76] *The Wanderer,* February 29, 1996.

[77] *Washington Times,* March 2, 1996.

[78] Ibid.

[79] Ibid.

[80] *American Renewal,* February 21, 1996.

[81] Ibid.

[82] Ibid.

[83] Ibid.

[84] Ibid.

[85] Ibid.

[86] Ibid.

[87] *The Wanderer,* Februrary 29, 1996.

CHAPTER 2

[1] Fulton, ed., *Roosevelt's Writings,* 168.

[2] *Atlantic Monthly,* February 1996.

[3] Patrick J. Buchanan, *Right from the Beginning* (Boston: Little, Brown & Co., 1988).

[4] *Atlantic Monthly,* February 1996.

[5] John Henry Newman, *The Idea of a University* (Chicago: Loyola University Press, 1927), vi.

[6] Ibid.

[7] Ibid.

[8] G. K. Chesterton, *Omnibus* (New York: Doran, 1953), 121.

[9] Barry Goldwater, *The Conscience of a Conservative* (Washington, D.C.: Regnery, 1990), x.

[10] Charles Lewis, *The Buying of the President* (New York: Avon, 1996), 95.

[11] *Media Alert,* March 15, 1996.

[12] Ibid.

[13] Ibid.

[14] *Newsweek,* March 4, 1996.

[15] Hilaire Belloc, *The Biographer's Art: Excerpts from Belloc's Florrid Pen* (London: Catholic Union, 1956), 33.

[16] Howard F. Pallin, ed., *Literary English and Scottish Sermons* (London: Windus Etheridge, 1937), 101.

[17] E. Michael Jones, *Degenerate Moderns: Modernity as Rationalized Sexual Misbehavior* (San Francisco: Ignatius Press, 1993), 9.

PART II/CHAPTER 3

[1] David L. Johnson, *Theodore Roosevelt: American Monarch* (Philadelphia: American History Sources, 1981), 44.

[2] Fulton, ed., *Roosevelt's Writings,* 179.

[3] *Newsweek,* March 4, 1996.

[4] *Time,* March 4, 1996.

[5] *U.S. News and World Report,* March 4, 1996.

[6] *Media Alert,* March 8, 1996.

[7] *Media Alert,* March 22, 1996.

[8] *Washington Times,* March 2, 1996.

[9] Marlin Maddoux, *Free Speech or Propaganda? How the Media Distorts the Truth* (Nashville, Tenn.: Thomas Nelson, 1990), 13.

[10] *The New American,* February 22, 1993.

[11] *Texas Education Review,* December 1992.

[12] *Media Alert,* March 22, 1996.

[13] Ibid.

[14] *Notable Quotables,* October 12, 1992.

[15] *Media Alert,* March 8, 1996.

[16] Ibid.

[17] Ibid.

[18] *C-Span,* February 20, 1993.

[19] *The Texas Education Review,* September 1992.

[20] *Media Alert,* March 22, 1996.

[21] *Convention Watch,* July 13, 1992.

[22] Ibid.

[23] Ibid.

[24] Ibid.

[25] Ibid.

[26] Ibid.

[27] Ibid.

[28] Ibid.

[29] Ibid.

[30] Ibid.

[31] Ibid.

[32] Ibid.

[33] Ibid.

[34] Ibid.

[35] Ibid.

[36] Neil Postman and Steve Powers, *How to Watch TV News* (New York: Penguin Press, 1992), 15.

[37] Alvin Toffler, *Future Shock* (New York: Bantam, 1971), 155.

[38] Postman and Powers, *How to Watch TV News,* 14.

[39] Ibid., 19.

[40] Ibid., 23.

[41] Herbert Collier and Wilbur Jones, *The Scandal of the "New Age" and the "New Witness"* (Bedford, UK: Distributist Press, 1966), 34–36, 41.

[42] Benson Hargraves, Lloyd Musselmann, and Leslie Offerdahl, *The Modern Leviathan: Pop Culture and Behavior in the Modern World* (London: Cranston and Hughes, 1991), 43–46.

[43] Ibid.

[44] Francis A. Schaeffer, *How Should We Then Live?* (Wheaton, Ill.: Crossway Books, 1975), 242–43.

[45] Donald Donaldson, *I'll Take My Stand: The South and the Agrarian Tradition* (Baton Rouge, La.: Louisiana State University, 1930), 176.

[46] Daniel Boorstin, *The Image: A Guide to Pseudo-Events in America* (New York: Atheneum, 1961), 7.

[47] Ibid., 8.

[48] Ibid.

[49] Jack Mingo and John Javna, *Primetime Proverbs* (New York: Harmony, 1989), 221.

[50] Ibid.

[51] Edward J. Epstein, *Between Fact and Fiction: The Problem of Journalism* (New York: Vintage Books, 1975), 3.

[52] Ibid., 4.

[53] Ibid.

[54] Ibid.

[55] Schaeffer, *How Should We Then Live,* 240.

[56] *Media Alert,* March 15, 1996.

[57] Ibid.

[58] James Srodes and Arthur Jones, *Campaign 1996* (New York: HarperCollins, 1996), 110.

59 Ibid.
60 *Media Alert,* March 15, 1996.
61 Ibid.
62 Ibid.
63 Ibid.
64 Ibid.
65 Ibid.
66 Ibid.
67 Ibid.
68 Ibid.
69 *USA Today,* January 28, 1993.
70 *Notable Quotables,* February 15, 1993.
71 *Notable Quotables,* January 4, 1993.
72 *Notable Quotables,* October 12, 1992.
73 *Notable Quotables,* January 4, 1993.
74 Ibid.
75 *Houston Chronicle,* August 23, 1992.
76 *World,* March 2, 1996.
77 Postman and Powers, *How to Watch TV News,* 104.
78 Ibid.
79 Jimmy Breslin, *Damon Runyon: A Life* (New York: Dell-Laurel, 1991), 2.
80 Ibid.
81 Ibid.
82 H. L. Mencken, *A Carnival of Buncombe* (Chicago: University of Chicago, 1980), 69.
83 Ibid.

CHAPTER 4

1 Roosevelt, *The Foes of Our Own Household,* 132.
2 *Media Alert,* March 8, 1996.
3 *Time,* March 4, 1996.
4 *Media Alert,* March 8, 1996.
5 Ibid.
6 Ibid.
7 Ibid.
8 Ibid.
9 Ibid.
10 Ibid.
11 Ibid.
12 Ibid.

[13] Ibid.
[14] Ibid.
[15] Ibid.
[16] Ibid.
[17] Ibid.
[18] Ibid.
[19] *Weekly Standard,* March 11, 1996.
[20] Ibid.
[21] *Media Alert,* March 8, 1996.
[22] Ibid.
[23] Ibid.
[24] *Los Angeles Times,* February 28, 1996.
[25] Ibid.
[26] Ibid.
[27] Ibid.
[28] *Atlantic Monthly,* December 31, 1995.
[29] *Weekly Standard,* November 27, 1995.
[30] Ibid.
[31] *Media Alert,* March 8, 1996.
[32] Ibid.
[33] Ibid.
[34] Ibid.
[35] *Media Alert,* February 2, 1996.
[36] Ibid.
[37] Ibid.
[38] Ibid.
[39] Ibid.
[40] Ibid.
[41] *Media Alert,* February 16, 1996.
[42] Ibid.
[43] Ibid.
[44] Ibid.
[45] *New York Times,* February 28, 1996.
[46] Ibid.
[47] Ibid.
[48] Ibid.
[49] Ibid.
[50] *Congressional Quarterly,* Winter 1995.
[51] Ibid.
[52] *Washington Post,* October 30, 1995.
[53] Ibid.
[54] Ibid.

[55] *World,* March 9, 1996.
[56] Ibid.
[57] *Face the Nation,* August 23, 1992.
[58] *Media Alert,* February 2, 1996.
[59] C. S. Lewis, *Mere Christianity* (New York: Macmillan, 1952).
[60] John Stott, *Basic Christianity* (Downers Grove, Ill.: InterVarsity Press, 1971).
[61] William Wilberforce, *Real Christianity* (Portland, Ore.: Multnomah, 1982).
[62] H. Lyndon Kilmer, *Helen Keller* (New York: Skillen and Fortas, 1964), 164.
[63] *Media Alert,* February 23, 1996.
[64] Buchanan Campaign lit at www.buchanan.org.
[65] Ibid.
[66] Ibid.
[67] Ibid.
[68] Ibid.
[69] Ibid.
[70] Ibid.
[71] Ibid.
[72] Ibid.
[73] Ibid.
[74] Ibid.
[75] Ibid.
[76] Ibid.
[77] Ibid.
[78] Ibid.
[79] Ibid.
[80] Ibid.
[81] Ibid.
[82] Ibid.
[83] Ibid.
[84] Ibid.
[85] Ibid.
[86] Ibid.
[87] Ibid.
[88] Ibid.
[89] *Washington Times,* March 2, 1992.

CHAPTER 5

[1] David L. Johnson, *Theodore Roosevelt: American Monarch* (Philadelphia: American History Sources, 1981), 91.

2 *Weekly Standard,* March 11, 1996.

3 Ibid.

4 Ibid.

5 *Chronicles,* February 1996.

6 Russell Kirk, ed., *The Portable Conservative Reader* (New York: Penguin, 1982), xv.

7 Ibid.

8 Ibid., xvi.

9 Ibid., xvi–xvii.

10 Ibid., xvii.

11 Ibid., xvii–xviii.

12 David Hall, ed., *Caveat: Welfare Reformed* (Franklin, Tenn.: Legacy Communications, 1993), 67.

13 G. K. Chesterton, *G. F. Watts* (New York: E. P. Dutton, 1901), 110.

14 Eric Voegelin, *Omnibus* (Jackson, Miss.: The Southern Company, 1969), 23.

15 Ibid., 45.

16 Ibid.

17 Ibid., 56.

18 Ibid.

19 Ibid., 97.

20 Michael Franz, *Ideology and Eric Voegelin* (Baton Rouge, La.: Louisiana State University Press, 1991), 34.

21 Horton Kael and William Loomis, *A Documentary History of Liberal Thought* (New York: M. H. Cushman's Publishing House, 1959), 246.

22 H. G. Wells, *What Is Coming?* (New York: Macmillan, 1916), 1–2.

23 Eric Voegelin, *Ideology: A Voegelin Anthology* (Zachary, La.: Free Dias, 1979), 55.

24 Ibid., 163.

25 Ibid., 228.

26 Ibid., 163.

27 William Peay Johnson, *The Development of an International Party* (London: Grovenor, 1979), 31.

28 Patricia Hollis, *Catholic Social Policy* (Minneapolis: Sisters of Charity, 1983), 46.

29 Kael and Loomis, *History of Liberal Thought,* 246.

30 Hollis, *Catholic Social Policy,* 48.

31 Ibid., 50.

32 Ibid., 49.

[33] Steven Rolle Davis, *The Southern Agrarians* (Jackson, Miss.: Southern, 1965), 5.

[34] Johnson, *International Party*, 33.

[35] Kael and Loomis, *History of Liberal Thought*, 244.

[36] Davis, *The Southern Agrarians*, 5.

[37] Hollis, *Catholic Social Policy*, 49.

[38] Johnson, *International Party*, 36.

[39] Ibid.

[40] Hollis, *Catholic Social Policy*, 44.

[41] Kael and Loomis, *History of Liberal Thought*, 249.

[42] Davis, *The Southern Agrarians*, 7.

[43] Johnson, *International Party*, 81.

[44] Hollis, *Catholic Social Policy*, 45.

[45] Ibid., 46.

[46] Kael and Loomis, *History of Liberal Thought*, 200.

[47] Davis, *The Southern Agrarians*, 7.

[48] Hollis, *Catholic Social Policy*, xii.

[49] Woodrow Wilson, *The New Freedom* (New York: Doubleday, Page, and Company, 1913), 3.

[50] Ibid.

[51] Ibid., 7.

[52] Ibid.

[53] Ibid., 4.

[54] Ibid.

[55] Ibid., 76.

[56] Ibid., 35.

[57] Ibid., 48.

[58] Ibid., 50.

[59] Ibid.

[60] Ibid., 14.

[61] Jacob Riis, *Theodore Roosevelt: The Citizen* (New York: Macmillan, 1904), 201.

[62] Ibid.

[63] Ibid., 285.

[64] Roosevelt, *Foes of Our Own Household*, 97.

[65] Riis, *Theodore Roosevelt*, 285.

[66] Thomas H. Russell, *The Political Battle of 1912* (New York: L. H. Walter, 1912), 204.

[67] Ibid.

[68] Ibid., 205.

[69] Ibid., 93.

[70] Clarence Carson, *The Growth of America* (Greenville, Ala.: American Textbook Committee, 1981), 235.

PART III/CHAPTER 6

[1] Roosevelt, *The Foes of Our Own Household*, 47.

[2] Archibald Roosevelt, ed., *Race, Riots, Reds, and Crime* (New York: Roosevelt Memorial Association, 1939), 101.

[3] *Media Alert,* March 8, 1996.

[4] James Branson, *A Documentary History of the United States* (New York: Grollier and Thames, 1969), 43.

[5] Ibid., 66.

[6] Ibid., 67.

[7] Ibid.

[8] G. K. Chesterton, *What I Saw in America* (New York: Dodd, Mead, 1922), 7.

[9] Ibid.

[10] Ibid.

[11] Ibid., 68.

[12] Ibid.

[13] Ibid.

[14] Ibid., 98.

[15] Harold K. Lane, *Liberty! Cry Liberty!* (Boston: Lamb and Lamb Tractarian Society, 1939), 31.

[16] Ibid., 32.

[17] Abraham Lincoln, *Complete Speeches, Letters, and Papers: 1860–1865* (Washington, D.C.: Capitol Library, 1951), 341–42.

[18] Gregory Suriano, ed., *Great American Speeches* (New York: Gramercy, 1993), 4.

[19] P. J. O'Rourke, *Parliament of Whores* (New York: Atlantic Monthly Press, 1991), 9.

[20] Donald Davidson, ed., *I'll Take My Stand* (Baton Rouge, La.: Louisiana State University, 1930), 201.

[21] Ibid., xlvi.

[22] Ibid., xx.

[23] Ibid., xv.

[24] Ibid., 75.

[25] Ibid., 88.

[26] Ibid.

[27] Ibid.

[28] Ibid.

[29] Ibid., xli.

[30] Ibid.

31 Ibid., 115.
32 Ibid., xl.
33 Ibid., xxxiii.
34 Ibid., 29.
35 Ibid., xliii.
36 Ibid., 5.
37 Ibid., xxx–xxxi.
38 Ibid.
39 Romans 1:18–22.
40 1 Corinthians 1:23.
41 Peter Jackson, *The Southern Agrarians* (Nashville, Tenn.: Franklin Publishing, 1955), 126.
42 Ibid., 184.
43 Ibid., 212.
44 *The Limbaugh Letter,* December 1992.
45 Ibid.
46 *Gallup Poll,* January 1993.
47 *Wirthlin Poll,* January 1993.
48 *American Demographic Report,* February 1993.
49 Ibid.
50 *National Review,* December 14, 1992.
51 Ibid.
52 Ibid.
53 *American Demographic Report,* February 1993.
54 *Austin American-Statesman,* November 26, 1992.
55 Ibid.
56 *Human Events,* November 21, 1992.
57 *USA Today,* July 14, 1995.
58 *Nashville Banner,* January 25, 1993.
59 Ibid.
60 Ibid.
61 Howard Phillips, *Caveat: Where Do We Go From Here?* (Franklin, Tenn.: Legacy Communications, 1993).
62 *Newsweek,* February 8, 1993.
63 Eric Felten, *The Ruling Class: Inside the Imperial Congress* (Washington, D.C.: Heritage Foundation, 1993).
64 G. K. Chesterton, *Omnibus* (London: Stratford Lewes, 1966), 142–43.
65 Mencken, *Quotations,* 41.
66 Bessie Blackstone Coleman, Willis L. Uhl, and James Fleming Hosic, *The Pathway Reader* (New York: Silver, Burdett, and Co., 1926), 107.

About the Author

George Grant is the director of the King's Meadow Study Center, the editor of the *Arx Axiom* newsletter, a regular columnist for both *World* and *Table Talk* magazines, the editorial director for Highland Books, and a teaching fellow at the Franklin Classical School. He is the author of more than three dozen books in the areas of politics, history, and social issues, including profiles of organizations such as Planned Parenthood, the American Civil Liberties Union, and the National Education Association and of individuals such as Alan Keyes, Ross Perot, Margaret Sanger, and Hilary Clinton. His most recent book is a biography of Theodore Roosevelt, *Carry a Big Stick*.

Over the years, Dr. Grant has served as a radio and television commentator, political campaign consultant, editorial director for four major publishing companies, and executive director for two national media outreach ministries. In addition to his regular classes in history, literature, and the arts at the Franklin Classical School, he maintains an active speaking schedule in this country and around the world.

He has studied political science at the University of Houston, theology at Midwestern Seminary, and literature and philosophy at Whitefield College and makes his home on a small farm in Tennessee with his wife and three children.

For information about the King's Meadow Study Center, its publications, and its various educational programs, contact:

King's Meadow Study Center
P.O. Box 1601
Franklin, TN 37065